Taking Root
in the Heart

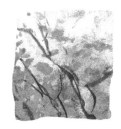

Taking Root
in the Heart

A Collection of Thirty-Four Poets
from *The Christian Century*

EDITED BY JILL PELÁEZ BAUMGAERTNER

IRON
PEN

PARACLETE PRESS
BREWSTER, MASSACHUSETTS

2023 First Printing

Taking Root in the Heart: A Collection of Thirty-Four Poets from The Christian Century
Copyright © 2023 by Jill Pelaez Baumgaertner

ISBN 978-1-64060-703-3

The Iron Pen name and logo are trademarks of Paraclete Press.

The poems in this book are reproduced here with the permission of *The Christian Century*, with the exception of "Beginning with the Crucifixion," which is reproduced here with the permission of Yehiel E. Poupko.

Library of Congress Cataloging-in-Publication Data

Names: Baumgaertner, Jill P., editor.
Title: Taking root in the heart : a collection of thirty-four poets from
  the Christian Century / edited by Jill Peleaz Baumgaertner.
Description: Brewster, Massachusetts : Paraclete Press, 2023. | Summary:
  "What defines all the poems in this collection is a commitment to
  communicating with readers seeking truth, beauty, and authenticity"--
  Provided by publisher.
Identifiers: LCCN 2022051193 (print) | LCCN 2022051194 (ebook) | ISBN
  9781640607033 | ISBN 9781640607040 (epub) | ISBN 9781640607057 (pdf)
Subjects: LCSH: Christian poetry, American. | BISAC: POETRY / Anthologies
  (multiple authors) | POETRY / American / General | LCGFT: Poetry.
Classification: LCC PS595.C47 T35 2023 (print) | LCC PS595.C47 (ebook) |
  DDC 811.008/03823--dc23/eng/20221101
LC record available at https://lccn.loc.gov/2022051193
LC ebook record available at https://lccn.loc.gov/2022051194

10 9 8 7 6 5 4 3 2 1

Published by Paraclete Press
Brewster, Massachusetts
www.paracletepress.com
Printed in the United States

For David Heim, John Buchanan, and Peter Marty

■

Let your feet move to the rhythm of your pulse
(Your joints like pearls and rubies he has hidden),
And your hands float high on the tide of your feelings.
Now, shout from the stomach, hoarse with music,
Give gladness and joy back to the Lord,
Who, sly as a milkweed, takes root in your heart.

—Robert Siegel, "Rinsed with Gold, Endless,
Walking the Fields"

CONTENTS

Malcolm Guite

Jeff Gundy

Charles Hughes

Jean Janzen

Philip C. Kolin

Sydney Lea

Karen An-Hwei Lee

Marjorie Maddox

Warren L. Molton

Julie L. Moore

Angela Alaimo O'Donnell

Steven Peterson

Yehiel E. Poupko

Shari Wagner

Jeanne Murray Walker

Paul Willis

Christian Wiman

Carl Winderl

INTRODUCTION

Let him easter in us, be a dayspring to the dimness of us,
be a crimson-cresseted east.
—Gerard Manley Hopkins, "The Wreck of the Deutschland"

Since 1884 the *Christian Century* has included poetry in its pages of religious news, theological and cultural reflection, and reviews of current books, films, and music. It is not unique in doing so. From *America* to *Anglican Theological Review* to the *Cresset* to *First Things* to almost every other major Christian publication of some repute, poetry finds its way into the pages. When asked why he wanted poetry in *First Things*, then editor Father Richard John Neuhaus replied, "Because it's classy." I wouldn't deny that it is classy. But I'd reach beyond appearance and impression and the ways in which a poem might adorn a page to point to William Carlos Williams, who said, "It is difficult to get the news from poems, yet men die miserably every day for lack of what is found there." A poem may be about what happened, but in describing what did happen, it should also point us to what does happen, what shouldn't happen, and what will happen. In the particular is the universal, so many writers have claimed, and that is what I as poetry editor seek: the individual experience or insight or description that strikes a nerve and will continue to strike nerves through the decades because it is true to the human in all of us.

When I first envisioned this project, I sought representative poems from the past one hundred years of the *Christian Century*. As I read through the brittle pages of past issues, I discovered that yes, indeed, the editors had looked for and published quality poetry—mainly reprints of poems by Christina Rossetti, Henry Wadsworth Longfellow, Carl Sandburg, Sara Teasdale, Sydney Lanier, and

George MacDonald—even a W. H. Auden poem in 1966. What I discovered in less well-known contributors was fascinating for archaeological and historical reasons, not necessarily aesthetic or theological. These poems were snapshots of culture and cultural concerns—for example, "Coffee at Howard Johnson's" (1970) or early feminist antiwar poems like S. J. Duncan-Clarke's "Women and War" (1915), a modern version of *Lysistrata*.

> O wombs refuse to bear,
>> O breasts refuse to nurse,
> Until thy sons who toil shall dare
>> To end this age-long curse!

Then there was "A Ballad of Bethlehem Steel" (1915), written by "The Public" with a gripe to air.

> A fort is taken, the papers say,
>> Five thousand dead in the murderous deal.
> A victory? No, just another grim day.
>> But—up to five hundred goes Bethlehem Steel.

During the Cold War, the poem "A Fallout Shelter Is Our God" appeared. Then nineteen days after President Kennedy was shot, the magazine published four poems by Manfred A. Carter, a Methodist minister—an unusually fast turnaround for poems, which usually require weeks and months through many revisions, and these four could have used some revision. In 1967, at the height of the Vietnam War, appeared "While Proctoring a Selective Service College Qualification Exam" by Judson Scruton.

> Today, students fear dying.
> There is no drone of teachers to comfort their need.
> No bread. No wine. Not even cigarettes.

"Your answers should be soft enough
To be smeared for electronic processing,
But stay firmly within the prescribed grid."

I was thrilled to discover John Updike's most-quoted poem in sermons, "Seven Stanzas at Easter," which appeared first in the *Christian Century* in 1961. He had written it for a Lutheran congregation in Massachusetts, and a pastor there had suggested the *Christian Century* as a possible publication site for it. Somewhere in the typesetting, a comma was omitted, and Updike vowed never to publish in the *Century* again. Fifty years later, a painstakingly accurate copy editor still referred to this mistake with deep regret. When I pulled that volume of the magazine off the shelves in the *Century* library and found the poem, someone had inked in a tiny comma on the fateful line. I imagine it was that dear and tortured copy editor.

I also found some disturbing content. One poet, dedicating a poem to Vassar Miller, the poet who suffered from cerebral palsy, described her as a "spastic spinster." A poem published in the 1920s during Jim Crow shows that sad influence, and another published in 1965 does some strong virtue signaling on the race issue, even while using, repetitively and supposedly ironically, a racist epithet. On the other hand, a long poem by Robert P. Desch, published in November 1968, feels achingly familiar. It could have been written this year. "Elegy at the Seventeenth Green" begins:

We wait at the first tee and swing hard at dandelions
Or book match covers, impatient for our turn.
I didn't know that King was shot.
Yesterday at work nobody said a thing.
What a shame!

Think of what the extremists will do.
Come on. We're up.

The poem continues as the golfers play hole after hole:

Martin Luther King lies dead as we hit on the second hole,
A slight dogleg to the right downhill.
Another slice—you're coming across the ball.
It's the first time out this year. Your game will come around in time.
There are people who say it takes time, only time, only time.
Only time doesn't solve any problem. It's neutral. It's blank.
And the forces of hate have used time more effectively, time
More efficiently, time to a greater advantage than those
Of good will who have wrung helpful hands as whole lifetimes
    were robbed
From the warehouse of freedom for year after year after year.
Damn it, another bad iron shot. Stay out of the trap!

Toward the end of the poem these prescient lines:

Weep white suburbs; let God hear your groan
Or rather let the bondsman hear, for God
Knows well your Adam guilt defined again
In Galilee at Wittenberg at Birmingham.
Let wailing rise like riot smoke:
From ashes spitting still white sparks of hate,
From store fronts of hypocrisy,
From tenements of insecurity,
From rubble layered deep with never, no, and wait.

Then there are the poems that bend toward cruel expression of outrage. "Merry Christmas to the Ladies Society," published in 1966, ends with these lines:

Large-busted loyal Lutherans
Hear this:
You paint the cheeks of a corpse
And your silly delight at rosiness
Is revolting.
It is you who killed him with your
Kitchen-warm clean hands.
Millie kissing the milkman
Under the mistletoe
Keeps Christmas better than you.

Emily Dickinson's instruction to "tell all the truth but tell it slant" evidently didn't make an impression on this particular poet.

As I perused these many decades of poems, I began to see the value in limiting this collection to the best and most prolific poets of the past twenty-five years. For one thing, the quality of verse submitted to the magazine has been steadily increasing over the past decades. Even so, at least two of our authors included in this collection, Warren Molton and J. Barrie Shepherd, have published poems in the *Christian Century* over many decades, and their work retains the freshness evident in their early poems.

What I look for, hungrily, in the poems I love has developed over a lifetime of poetry reading, teaching, and editing for various journals. My earliest experience in poetry editing occurred in 1973 at the *Cresset*, published by Valparaiso University. In those years Ken Korby was the editor, and he hired me as a "poetry consultant" to attack the huge pile of poetry submissions that had accumulated and remained unread. What he required of me was work that some might consider tedious, but I loved the challenge of it. I was to read each author's work, create an index card with the names of the submitted poems, and rate each poem on a scale from 1 to 5, giving reasons for my rating. I learned more that year about what makes a good poem than I had picked up through all the years of my schooling. I have to admit that the standards I was finally able to articulate and uphold so many years ago have remained pretty consistent through the years. Korby promoted me to poetry editor, a position I held for fifteen years until moving with then *Cresset* editor Jim Nuechterlein to *First Things*. Then, in 1996, David Heim invited me to serve as poetry editor of the *Christian Century*, which is where I have happily remained ever since.

What do I look for in the poems I choose for publication? I am interested in poems which defy the narcissistic tendencies of so much contemporary poetry. I don't seek a particular orthodoxy, but I do want the poems to connect with something larger than the self. I search for poetry that attempts to revitalize language, especially theological language. I look for poems that attempt to upset the usual modes of expression and offer up new angles of vision, especially in regard to biblical stories. For most of our poets—though not all by any means (Rabbi Yehiel Poupko is a frequent contributor)—Jesus is the Word made flesh, and the Incarnation is the paradigm as poets attempt to enflesh the abstract. So I seek poems that make the spirit tangible and put into words the unsayable. Of course, that is ultimately impossible, isn't it? But poets have a way of taking on what utterly cannot be done. And those are the poems I want to appear in a journal of religious news and reflection.

A poem says, *Pay attention!* A poem brackets an experience and turns it upside down in order for us to see it right side up again. It surprises and upsets the usual. It uses rhythm and rhyme and all of the other sound effects the language provides—

alliteration, assonance, consonance—in all of the traditional and nontraditional poetic forms—sonnets, ghazels, sestinas, rondeaus, villanelles, free verse—to bring into focus suffering or beauty or fear or God's compelling presence. Or absence, as the case may be. Poetry tackles the big questions, sometimes pointing to tentative answers, sometimes offering more questions. Poetry, in short, is a kind of real presence—spirit and word and concrete images—a means of charity, clemency, and mercy even in the midst of anger and frustration and disillusion.

The poems I choose for publication often explore biblical themes, doctrinal issues, or theological conundrums. For poets of faith there are precious few outlets for these explorations, although journals like *Spiritus, Image, Presence, Windhover*, and others I have already mentioned do exceptional work in publishing poetry anchored in the Word. But many of the poems that appear in the *Christian Century* present human experience or encounters with the natural world that do not seem on the surface "religious" but reveal a deep humanity at the core. Jeanne Murray Walker's "Little blessing for a suicidal child" (p. 164), for example, describes a highway encounter "when a girl in a silver car aims / for me." The speaker feels "loathing" and "hatred" and then as she swerves, sees the flash of the child's face, "her suffering / frown, how exposed she is." The poem shows hate transformed to compassion as "a voice speaks through me: *May / her parents see her face alive / again.*" In a poem titled "The best poem *ever*," Brian Doyle, in his inimitable style, quotes a child who asks, "What if . . . / We made a poem without using any words at all?" The child continues: "Poems in / Books are only a little bit of all the poems there are. / Those are only the poems someone found words for." In "Sad little patriarch, rubbing his gloved hands together" (p. 28), Brett Foster writes about his struggle with chemo, which made the winter cold feel like "a tiny razor blade slicing the skin." His remedy is a winter mask, "all black- / hooded with eye slits," and he recognizes that

> If I were to wear the black hood,
> guise of a hangman (not the one hanged),
> I fear that campus security would target me,
> bucolic space locked down in emergency
> protocol. That's all I would be: self-terrorist,
> strapped with the various wires of my sickness.

But in what may appear to be a poem about the ravages of disease, there is the epigraph from Psalm 88. This is not an unusual occurrence in the poems we print. Our authors have a way of grounding their words and their experiences, no matter how secular they may seem, in the realm of the spiritual.

Of course, some of those groundings are overt and pervasive. Anya Silver wrote "Psalm 137 for Noah" (p. 144) after being diagnosed with metastatic breast cancer during her pregnancy. The cancer finally took her life fourteen years later, her voice resonant and convicting in the poems she left behind. In this poem she writes to her son, Noah:

> Come darling, sit by my side and weep.
> I have no lyre, no melodious voice or chant.
> I meditate on the Zion I could never grant you.
> My son, my roe deer, my rock-rent stream.
> My honeysuckle, my salt, my golden spear.
> Forgive me your birth in this strange land.

In Jill Alexander Essbaum's "A good Christian mustn't fear the darkness of the grave" (p. 24), the reader is plunged into the ground with the corpse.

You are appalled, shrouded,
sutured shut. They did not put the pillow in between
your knees. And, your lipstick's smeared. Once upon,

you wished for a thousand infinities. Finally arrived,
nothing can be more broken, nothing can be more
than dead. To the uncarved side of your stone,

a devil tree bends. But this, of course, is not the end.

Rabbi Yehiel Poupko's poems are anchored firmly in the Torah and in Jewish experience, including the Holocaust. In "Beginning with the crucifixion" (p. 109) he writes of the crucifixion in a chilling new context.

and we
thought,
alright
he's only
one Jew
let them
have their
just one Jew,
appetite satisfied
with just one Jew
and we'll
be saved, and having had one
just one Jew
appetite grew
and grew
for one
more Jew. . . .

The poetic approaches and styles of the work of these poets are immensely varied, from the masterful narratives of Sydney Lea to the finely wrought lyrics of Charles Hughes to the always edgy and surprising poems of Bill Stadick to the most imagistic and prolific work of Luci Shaw to the challenging and provocative words of Christian Wiman. Then there are the superb sonnets of Gracia Grindal, Malcolm Guite, and Angela Alaimo O'Donnell and the compelling explorations of the deep spirituality of the everyday that comprise Tania Runyan's vision. In the past few years we have lost four of our poets—Kim Bridgford, Anya Silver, Brett Foster, and Brian Doyle—to cancer, but we will never lose their voices.

The poets chosen for this collection have published many poems in the journal over the past twenty-five years. I have had to omit many others who deserve to appear here but whose work has not appeared as often. To all of the poets who have published in the *Christian Century*, I send a huge thank-you for trusting us with your work and for making us look good, week after week. I owe a huge debt of gratitude to the three colleagues to whom I dedicate this collection: To David Heim, the executive editor of the *Christian Century* until 2020, who provided all of his staff with a model of the engaged and committed life and whose words have power because he is a quiet man who knows when to be bold. To John Buchanan, publisher of the *Christian Century* for so many years, and to Peter Marty, current editor and publisher, I am indebted for their wise leadership, their solid understanding of the Word, and their love of poetry. I am grateful to Janice Potter and to Rachel Pyle, editorial assistants par excellence, who helped with all of the sundry tasks that have come with this project; to Amy Frykholm and Elizabeth Palmer, who were enthusiastic encouragers from the beginning; and to Steve Thorngate, whom I have watched from his earliest student days to his current position as managing editor, where he always says yes to my increasing desire for more space for poems, which somehow gracious art director Dan Richardson always finds. Siobhan Drummond has provided invaluable service on the mechanics of this manuscript and with eagle-eyed copyediting, and she has become the friend every poet needs. Heidi Baumgaertner has supported this project with her usual brilliant and creative promotional advice.

At Paraclete my patient and wise editor, Robert Edmonson, kept me grounded and encouraged. Rachel McKendree is the publicist *par excellence* whose enthusiasm and energy fuels every project she promotes.

As always, Martin has been the spouse every poet should have—generous with encouragement, patient, and quite naturally judicious—and has proven through the years that, as John Donne wrote, "Love is a growing, or full constant light."

Kim Bridgford

KARMA

By the end, you will have suffered from it all:
At first you didn't understand why people
That you worked with would think about you, quibble
With how you lived your life. Now you know fall
And rise, how a life has more to do with lies.
How jealousy is understandable,
Revenge the toothpick in the gums, to trouble
Even you. There is a bitterness in ways
Of seeing: those heavy, layered wines; the bread
Poisoned. *Come, sit down. My favorite is the crust.*
It's not that the last supper was the last;
It was the day that it revealed that even
The good guys were impure. How they were lost
And resisted giving up what they were given.

PETER

You were that kind of guy. The kind to think
That you were better than the others. That's
The curse, you see. I knew that you would blame
Circumstances and the atmosphere.
That's how it is: You are what you most fear.
You think you know your shining, private name:
You don't. It is the language of your secrets.
You couldn't believe that you'd deny. To think

That this was you! Inside your robes, the feeling
Of guilt that shamed; your goodness was inferred.
You have many ways to shape how you are weak.
For example, you must bear the blame, the word
You know you didn't say. This is your failing.
Yet God gives you a do-over, once you speak.

YOU CAN'T GO BACK

"You can't go back," my mother always said.
But human nature does the opposite.
(Of course, this happens, but inside your head.)

Unspill your coffee? Leave your words unsaid?
The jeans from years ago will suddenly fit!
"You can't go back," my mother always said,

And she was right. The dead are not undead,
And traumas still will need a tourniquet.
(Of course, this happens, but inside your head.)

You want your moments cut and edited.
You want the bliss, and not the deep regret.
"You can't go back," my mother always said.

The trick is to remember what you had
And simultaneously forgive, forget.
(Of course, this happens, but inside your head.)

It is never quite in balance, this method
Of loving who you were, and you aren't yet.
"You can't go back," my mother always said.
(Of course, this happens, but inside your head.)

AT THE TOMB II

His offering made us see what could be done
With flesh and blood. First, we had eaten from
His gestures—wine and bread—and what we'd been
Was gone. We knew that we belonged to him.

Then, waiting with our grief beside the tomb,
We were made humble, and our faces wet.
We wanted his return; we wanted *him*,
The way he made our truth immediate.

But he was gone, and what would happen now?
We felt the loss that he'd inherited,
The loss we'd given him, that pierced him through.
There, we were bound by all that wasn't said.

And, finally, realizing what was known,
We closed our eyes, and saw him rise through stone.

LAZARUS
Fishers of men

Because you found me somewhere in-between,
Because you realized the truth of that,
You pulled me up. The not-seen was now seen—

Like something that's half-buried, serpentine,
A vine the wind has covered, dust unset—
Because you found me. Somewhere in-between,

The insects covered me in celebration,
And God began to pull, from where He sat.
You pulled me too. The not-seen was now seen:

The end-result a case of God-confusion.
Because who else could do a thing like that?
Because you found me somewhere in-between,

God stepped aside, for you, and it was done.
And so the grave-clothes, and your welcome mat.
Pull me up. The not-seen was now seen.

Who would have thought? The son in imitation:
And I come stumbling out into the sunlight.
Because you found me somewhere in-between,
You pulled me up, like roots, as was foreseen.

Peter Cooley

COLUMBARIUM

I. Front

After mass, every Sunday in the churchyard
I've come to visit you, touch the weatherings
along the roseate stone carved with your name,
birthdate, death date. Then with my fingertips
I drop a kiss along the façade, pretending you're inside.

II. Sides

Sometimes my fingers slip, I brush my waiting place
below or next to you, I'm not sure which.
"That check includes you, too, Peter," Father Jim said,
his faith in immortality, melodious, monotonous,
a little concerto for violin and cello.

III. Back

You're no more there than are here,
where, when, I go to find you, these revenants
haunting the top drawer of the dresser.
Multicolored panties, I bought you holidays,
those pearls caught in your engagement picture.

IV. Top

Next Sunday, maybe, I'll skip a visit.
Why try to find you when you're always
shadow and light intertwined beside me,
day-night, sun-moon, their syncopations
unasked for, random grace I can't answer.

A STRAND OF PEARLS

A single lamentation, I'm done?
No, just a different one, to name the rains,

tintinnabulation at the window,
the bent lament of morning's radiance

refusing to appear at this blue glass
where last night I could reach out, name the stars,

many, many my imaginations.
Where are the pearls you wore in your engagement photo

watching me from the piano as I pass by,
piano you played until the end, even half-blind.

These pearls—the girl who wore them stands right now
beside me, mere seconds, in this prayer-poem.

Seconds. God, the cruelty of prayer.

BARCAROLLE

The day I was confirmed, you turned to me,
sang out, while I stared straight ahead
through the sudden Wisconsin blizzard,

trying to keep our car on course toward home,
"Maybe this is why we got together."
I thought that was too much hindsight, foresight.

Now, ten months into your death, our life
together winds and unwinds, spiraling,
snowdrifting, melting, freezing to melt again.

On the west wall of the room you smoked in,
coughed through, smoked, room I've had repainted
that blue the sky aspires to, our cross

we bought together at the Poor Clare's Bazaar,
our cross holds up these words you've brought to me.
Hanging it back up in the repainted room,

after the fumigation and new hue,
I chipped the paint, the plaster. The cross—
it waits for me to finish singing this. The cross—

The cross gives me new words, to call them mine,
to draw from currents of this morning room.
The cross is still not finished with us yet.

The cross stares down at me, a still, unfinished look.

NOW,

after a first moment in eternity
I turn around. I'm back in my backyard,
the weeping willow dead, the bottle brush,
the southern flowers I planted, novelties
to me, the northerner, dead, dead, all dead.

And on the branches of the dead magnolia
the dead birds perch, swallow and nightingale,
their dead eyes holding reflections of the flowers,
genus and species, dead, sere, leaves cracked, dead
all crawling things, all flying, speechless, dead,

waiting and hollowed out with harrowing.
I lay my hand among these shadowings.
Because she always answered, I choose her,
this mockingbird. I sing her my first word.
The rest is heaven, endlessness of grace,

the skyline of the backyard limitless,
my old broken eloquence of song aligned
with certain resurrection's aftermath,
this minute to be repeated and repeated
repeated and repeated my bird sings.

Rembrandt,
"The Woman Taken in Adultery"
National Gallery, Trafalgar Square, London

Just as I came out of the Gallery,
I saw a gull among hordes of tourists
encircling the statue of Lord Nelson,
crazed while I prayed he'd make it out, resume
flight I attribute to all birds, boundless.

But my dying: I try to keep it lined
around the edges of the ordinary
so I can—shall I say—appreciate?

Drawn to that picture by the glowing dark
around the woman, kneeling, Christ standing,
the Scribes and Pharisees shrouded in black,
I saw she, too, has just discovered light,
knowing, moments ago, she escaped stoning.

She just this instant came to where I'm going.

Michelangelo, *Pietà*

Hewn from some polar
air they make us breathe
just to look on here,
they appear doubles,
Michelangelo,
son, mother, one death,

Christ, his body bent,
broken on her lap,
stretches beyond pain.
Mary, suffering
His death till her own
looks out, straight into us.

Why did I bear him?
How can this be mine?
You who have come from
where the living live,
what do mothers do?

Barbara Crooker

MURMURATION

Cold morning, November, taking a walk,
when up ahead, suddenly, the trees unleave,
and thousands of starlings lift off, an immense
river of noise; they braid and unbraid themselves
over my head, the gray silk sky embroidered
with black kisses, the whoosh of their wings,
their chattering clatter, patterns broken/formed/
reformed, a scarf of ragged ribbons. Dumb-
struck, mouth open, I say *holy* and I say *moly*.
And then, they're gone.

BOOK OF KELLS
October 19, 2013: folio 253v-254r

The text of the day is open to Luke, chapter sixteen,
verse ten. The initial N, made up of blond men

facing off, grappling and tugging at each other's beards,
becomes the first word in the section that warns us

that no servant can serve two masters. Irony intended.
Later, in beautiful insular majuscule, the open letters filled

in red and blue, we read *You cannot serve both god and money.*
I wish that these words would rise off the page, a swarm of bees,

become honey to spread on our daily bread. When the scribes
made an error, in a world before white-out, the correct word

was inserted in a box of red dots. Aren't there words today
we'd like to amend like that? In this dimly lit room, circling

glass cases, I return to view the same vellum over again.
Twelve hundred years later, clear as the day it was written,

I think of Henri Nouwen: *The word is born in silence,
and silence is the deepest response to the word.*

NARRATIVE

This morning's miracle: dawn turned up its dimmer,
set the net of frost on the lawn to shining. The sky,
lightly iced with clouds, stretched from horizon
to horizon, not an inch to spare, and later, the sun
splashed its bucket of light on the ground. But it's
never enough. The hungry heart wants more: another
ten years with the man you love, even though you've had
thirty; one more night rinsed in moonlight, bodies twisted
in sheets, one more afternoon under the plane trees
by the fountain, with a jug of red wine and bits of bread
scattered around. More, even though the dried grasses
are glowing in the dying light, and the hills are turning
all the syllables of lavender, as evening draws the curtains,
turns on the lamps. One more book, one more story,
as if all the words weren't already written, as if all the plots
haven't been used, as if we didn't know the ending already,
as if this time, we thought it could turn out differently.

DAY OF THE DEAD

November 1st, the veil thinner, and we remember
those who've gone to the other side. Don't worry,
I say, I'll be there soon. But for now, I mark the presence
of their absence, an ache in the throat, a finger
on memory's pulse. Light candles to keep out the dark,
to mark a path, should they wish to return. The floating world
shimmers and ebbs. I'd like to cross over, just for one hour,
see my mother, hold my baby, talk to Clare. Perched on our shoulders,
the dead ride with us, teetering like pyramids of water skiers, forming
enormous wings. Their words, though, remain inaudible. Cold syllables.
They scratch maps in frost on dark windows, but no one can read them.

Cross the threshold. This night is ancient and long. Whisper in my ear,
tell me what the new year will bring. Look at how the candle uses up
its wax. See how the smoke rises in the hearth.

EUONYMUS ALATUS

Outside my window, the bushes have turned, redder
than any fire, and the sky is the same blue Giotto
used for Mary's robes. My mother says if she still
had a house, she'd plant one or two of these bushes,
and I love how she's still thinking about gardening,
as if she were in the middle of the story, even though
we both know she's at the end. Down in the meadow,
the goldenrod's gone from cadmium yellow to a feathery
beige, the ghost of itself. Mother, too, fades away,
skin thin as the tissue stuffed up her sleeve.

The scars on her stomach itch and burn, but inside,
she's still the girl who loved to turn cartwheels, the woman
whose best days were on fairways and putting greens.
On television, we watch California go up in smoke,
flames leapfrogging ridge to ridge. Here, these leaves
release a shower of scarlet feathers, as everything starts
to let go. Oh, how this world burns and burns us,
yet we are not consumed.

Brian Doyle

GOD

By purest chance I was out in our street when the kindergarten
Bus mumbled past going slow and I looked up just as all seven
Kids on my side of the bus looked at me and I grinned and they
Lit up and all this crap about God being dead and where is God
And who owns God and who hears God better than whom is the
Most egregiously stupid crap imaginable because if you want to
See God and have God see you and have this mutual perception
Be completely untrammeled by blather and greed and comment,
Go stand in the street as the kindergarten bus murmurs past. I'm
Not kidding and this is not a metaphor. I am completely serious.
Everyone babbles about God but I saw God this morning just as
The bus slowed down for the stop on Maple Street. God was six
Girls and one boy with a bright green and purple stegosaurus hat.
Of course God would wear a brilliantly colored tall dinosaur hat!
If you were the Imagination that dreamed up everything that ever
Was in this blistering perfect terrible world, wouldn't you wear a
Hat celebrating some of the wildest most amazing developments?

A PERPLEX RAISING

The man on death row in the federal penitentiary writes to me
On lined loose-leaf paper that when he was a boy in the South
He was so absorbed by tent revivals that he knew he would be
A preacher, knew it in his deepest bones. I would stand on my
Bed and preach to the babies, and stand on a barrel and preach
To the chickens and the hogs, and preach the Word to the cow,
Who would not come to Jesus nor to anyone else neither. Well,
That is not how things turned out for me, which is a long story,
But what I want to get down in this letter is the blessings I had
When I was a boy. Now there is much to say that was not at all
In the least blessed, it was a violent and perplex raising we had,
But what I want to get down is that was a time of great wonder
And satisfaction for me because I knew what I was going to be.
I could spend a lot of time explaining how I came to not be that
Which I knew I was going to be but I have wasted enough time
In that fruitless pursuit. Thank you for reading this letter, which
Is a kindness on your part. It allowed me to remember a blessed
Time, there on the old barrel preaching the Word to the animals.

THE BEST POEM *ever*

What if, says a small child to me this afternoon,
We made a poem without using any words at all?
Wouldn't that be cool? You could use long twigs,
And feathers, or spider strands, and arrange them
So that people *imagine* what words could be there.
Wouldn't that be cool? So there's a different poem
For each reader. That would be the best poem *ever.*
The poem wouldn't be on the page, right? It would
Be in the air, sort of. It would be between the twigs
And the person's eyes, or *behind* the person's eyes,
After the person saw whatever poem he or she saw.
Maybe there are a *lot* of poems that you can't write
Down. Couldn't that be? But they're still there even
If no one can write them down, right? Poems in
Books are only a little bit of all the poems there are.
Those are only the poems someone found words for.

MRS. JOB

There was a man in the land of Uz, whose name was Job;
And he was essentially a blameless dude, and unarrogant,
And he was blessed with seven sons, and three daughters,
Which is a lot of children, and where, I ask politely, is the
Part of the Book of Job where we talk about Job's spouse,
Who is conspicuously not discussed in the back and forth
With his buddies and then suddenly the Big Guy Himself
Answering out of the whirlwind and commanding old Job
To gird up his loins, which loins were undeniably vigorous
Previous to the Lord interrupting Job, and after the Maker
Finishes one of the greatest eloquent scoldings of all time,
He grants old Job another seven sons and three daughters,
Again without the slightest thanks for the astounding Mrs.
Job who suddenly has twenty count them twenty children
With no mention of her humor, or the vast hills of diapers,
Or her wit which survived kids throwing up and the sheep
Wandering off, and plagues of locusts and things like that.
A good editor, I feel, would have asked for just a glancing
Nod to the wry hero of the tale, at least acknowledgment;
Something like a new last line after *So Job died, being old
and full of days,* which might read, And also passed a most
Amazing woman, of whom nothing other than the blessing
Was ever said, her heart being a gift beyond calculation by
Man, her mind sharp, her tongue gentle, her hands a mercy,
And her very presence full reason to kneel in prayer at that
Which the Lord in His mercy has made and granted briefly.
A line like that would only hint at her, but it's a start, right?

ASH WEDNESDAY

Here's your Ash Wednesday story.
A mother carries her tiny daughter
With her as she gets ashed and the
Girl, curious and wriggly, squirms
Into the path of the priest's thumb
Just as the finger is about to arrive
On the mother's forehead, and the
Ashes go right in the kid's left eye.
She starts to cry, and there's a split
Second as the priest and the mother
Gawk, and then they both burst out
Laughing. The kid is too little to be
Offended, and the line moves along,
But this stays with me; not the ashy
Eye as much as the instant when all
Could have been pain and awkward
But instead it led to mutual giggling.
We are born of dust and star-scatter
And unto this we shall return, this is
The Law, but meantime, by God, we
Can laugh our asses off. What a gift,
You know? Let us snicker while we
Can, brothers and sisters. Let us use
That which makes dark things quail.

Jill Alexander Essbaum

VARIETY OF HELLS

Hell: the inescapable presence of God endured in the permanent absence of Him.

A hell where your name is forgotten.
Worse, the hell that remembers you.
Every rotten scheme your hands laid plan to.

Then, a hell for omissive sins.
All what you meant to do though couldn't.
How you intended to love, but didn't.

A hell for revenge songs and ridicule.
A hell where despair is winnowed by fire.
A hell that burns away desire.

Hell of all hells: I harrow for your ghost.
But we abide eternities apart.
That's the hell of the heart.

O AFTERWARDS: A BENEDICTION

And may the old life, that rotting flesh and treasure,
find in the good pleasure

of Christ, a forgetfulness complete: That these sins, however
humanly deliberate my misbehaviors,

be blotted from the record of God, raptured like the night's thief,
forever gone, newly clean.

And may this new self shine like the moon shone long ago, before
she was rent by the devil's incisor,

a whole, round body not meant to be broken into phases.
And may she sing your praises

like Golgotha sings of a tree: For there is nothing empty
that cannot be filled. And may the sea

and all things swimming it thirst no longer for Living Water.
And may the Father

know the Daughter, even as the end of the earth unfolds.
And may I turn to gold.

CROSS

The branches of this tree
not broken, not bent—
but spent.

And no amount of tears
might drown the vacant
hole that rants

into hell. Three days, and
a sleep so catastrophically scarred
that nightmares mar

even the living landscape.
Who will rest in the City of Bread?
Soon, soon. The head's

already in the sky. Mercy
on the splinter and the thorn.
To die is to be born.

SAYS SOME ANGEL TO ONE MARY OR ANOTHER—

Not in the garden, not in the tomb,
not in the old shoe. Not in the furnace,
its resonance and heat. The telephone's signature

ring is silent now, no voice to carouse the tenor
and tremble of righter dreams. The rosebuds have
a clean finger to their lips—hush. He is not in the second hand,

which ticks upon itself. Hush—he's not in the second chance,
that old hope which stumbles like a nomad over the Reed Sea.
Indeed, the cellar door is locked and nothing sweet inside

but the perverse perseverance of jelly jars, red, wet cherries
from a spinster's finest branch. Taste and see: he's not
in the swallow, the tongue or the teeth. No one such as you desire,

here today. Oh Lady, look to otherwise, turn to Oz or Elsewhere,
juncture of M and 12 on a fantasized map. The he you seek
might shroud out upon an island for years and songs

under the perils of a kiss beneath an uncharted chair.
Or, open your palm to cradle something small and dear.
Perhaps he's there.

A GOOD CHRISTIAN MUSTN'T FEAR THE DARKNESS OF THE GRAVE

But let me tell you about its landscape. Small, hot, wooden,
and from above no one will hear you murmur *let me out.*
Out of the darkness nothing's delivered. Still, you beg it

to the brass of the coffin's creak hinge while satin
grows stench and your death dress rots away. You are livid
and left alone. The red jasper chaplet in your hand inclines

to the pretense of prayer. You are appalled, shrouded,
sutured shut. They did not put the pillow in between
your knees. And, your lipstick's smeared. Once upon,

you wished for a thousand infinities. Finally arrived,
nothing can be more broken, nothing can be more
than dead. To the uncarved side of your stone,

a devil tree bends. But this, of course, is not the end.

Brett Foster

WHAT EVER HAPPENED TO THE BABY JESUS?

Near chamomile and rosebud potpourri
a pair of porcelain camels rests, bit players
glazed and unaware of this faux Nativity.
Peasant extras lift their silent, pleasing prayers
with seasonal adoration. None harbors
signs of panic: no goats or stable maids,
no wise trio, those dazzled star readers
bearing gifts of frankincense and myrrh.
Not the puzzled carpenter from Galilee.
Not the curious shepherds, nor the virgin
exhausted still from her spotless labor.

These figures encircle a barren trough.
Where have you gone, O lost Christ child?
In truth, the Messiah's size is the stuff
of legend: he's been abducted. (No Ascension-
Come-Early before the ministry begins)
Not much bigger than a packing peanut,
the babe's become an object of devotion,
begotten for those tenacious paws' wild
swatting or mouth that totes the Savior in haste.
We spy the vacancy and know the culprit:
fat Larry, golden pear and roly-poly cat,

that ring-tailed and recidivist felon.
Regular brigand of the infant Son,
he mocks this fragile coffee-table cast.

We joke that his is a holy commission,
converting birthplace to an empty tomb,
Bethlehem yoking the born and risen.
Each time He's someplace new: laundry room
or water dish. Under chair, in basement,
unknown manger now. And still His grace
and tiny lacquered limbs feel ever present,
embodying their reliquaried space.

LONGING, LENTEN

The walk back, more loss. When I open the door
it's over, so I set to piddling: tidy
end tables, check the mail, draw a bath.
The restless energy finally settles
as I pass the mirror. I peer into it.
My nose touches glass. Not much left,
already effaced, not even a cross
to speak of. A smudge. A few black soot stains
like pinpoints on the forehead. The rest
of the blessed ash has vanished to a grey
amorphousness, to symbolize . . . not much.
Except a wish for those hallowed moments
to be followed by sustaining confidence.
Except spirit, which means to shun its listless
weight for yearning, awkward if not more earnest
prayer and fasting in the clear face of dust.

ON BEING ASKED TO PRAY

I think once again about your brother
and sister-in-law, god-awful uncertainty
as they await the news. I almost hear
their parental oath, or nearly so since
the legal process started with his birth,
this infant boy they're hoping to adopt
who's been exposed to heroin and meth.
How much so they don't know yet,
but expect the tox screens will soon appear,
announcing extent and consequence.

Till then their prayers are ample, open
to inscrutable will, yet not remotely serene.
The couple's caught up in their frequency.
Naturally they're solicitous to gain
everyone's lifted pleading, fruitful and keen.
So when asked if I will pray, I sense
it's the least, potently least, I can do
as they do their best outside the NICU.
So blessings upon your family, both
immediate and extended. (I mean

your family, but then again the prayers too,
lifted by air across hope's mezzanine.)

HARROWING & EXHILARATING

Your encouraging words of description feel just right
as I struggle to be heard, and work to remember
and depict this long summer month, which approached
like a soot-stained messenger fueling his miner's light
with pain and grief and fear. And yet what dynamite
remains here for me, defiant in a laughing gas chamber,
determined to retain a personal trainer, a shortened-life coach.

SAD LITTLE PATRIARCH, RUBBING HIS GLOVED HANDS TOGETHER

> *"I have been even as a man that hath no strength,*
> *free among the dead . . . Shall thy loving-kindness be*
> *showed in the grave?"*
> —Psalm 88

Some days I feel as old as father Abraham,
doddering father of a teen-aged daughter
who last week attended her first "real" concert,
at the crowded Aragon Ballroom in Uptown.
When will my own days feel real again,
the frozen clock hands begin to turn again?
When will this chemical burning in the veins
stop, and hope, perhaps, be recompensed?
I wear this long wool coat against the cold
that hurts me, covered with two scarves,
my face covered to avoid any feeling
of cobwebs, with their every thread feeling
like a tiny razor blade slicing the skin.

There is no ounce of benignity in this feeling.
Maybe that is why the winter mask,
last week found at Target, most accurately
resembles a terrorist accessory, all black-
hooded with eye slits. Were I to wear it,
I would appear on campus like an ISIS
recruit, no doubt a proud servant
in his mind, clouded by the violence
of the mission and sentence he honors.
O the necessary horrors, those airstrikes
occurring in the body's battleground, leveled
at the cells. If I were to wear the black hood,
guise of a hangman (not the one hanged),
I fear that campus security would target me,
bucolic space locked down in emergency
protocol. That's all I would be: self-terrorist,
strapped with the various wires of my sickness.

Nola Garrett

LEAVING

A 12 foot square of crime scene tape
stretches below my seventh floor window
where the tree trimmer plunged
to his death, after the oak branch,
carrying the squirrel nest
I've been admiring all fall—
a nursery confection built
of twigs and leaves, lined with moss
and feathers for warmth, meant to ride
the winds. The trimmer's father saw
his son die. That's the way it may have felt
for the nest makers. I should equate
both griefs, but I am not God,
only a human, a pattern maker
seeking to make sense of the senseless.

THE PASTOR'S WIFE CONSIDERS PURGATORY

My Pittsburgh son haunts thrift shops,
collects old rosaries, hangs them on nails
down cellar, near his bathroom door.

Buried with their best crystal rosaries,
crocheted among their fingers,
all those old ladies trouble me
when I consider how their every-day

rosaries were taken by their daughters
to be entombed in gold, pasteboard boxes,

until years later when their daughters
were readying for their move
to Florida (for the sake of the mover's bill)
lightened their load by donating the darker
contents of their dresser drawers to Goodwill.

THE PASTOR'S WIFE AND I

The pastor's wife does not go out to play.
Outside it is Tuesday—merciless and far

from Sunday. She is all righteous carrots
and earnest potatoes. Sometimes she hurts

me with her notions, makes my shoulders droop,
reminds me that Nola's dreams are a troop

of untrained monkeys. she recycles
my prayers, drags me away from dark angels.

But, when her hair grew prim and gray, I made
her dye it brown. Then, she chose our second husband,

a good man given to chills—him, I seduced.
Now, like a gun, she holds her watch

to my ear, forces me to write these poems.
It was I who fed her those wild greens,

a salad cut from my last of my pagan
garden's rue. Her mouth burns

for benedictions and shooting stars.
Into my mirror she stares, worries

I might disappear—her feral woman—
the woman who met Christ at the well.

THE PASTOR'S WIFE CONSIDERS GRAY

Am I a God near by says the Lord,
and not a God far off?
—Jeremiah 23:23

Some days Yahweh's crayon box
holds colors for tiptoes within regret's bold
lines, and others for scribbling acceptance's
Wild Blue Yonder on bathroom walls,

jet trails through every grown-up's sky. Silver
becomes the dime I find in Seven Eleven's
parking lot, the memory of a minnow's flash
or Aunt Mary's lost ring—found.

And there's *this* gray crayon's violet wrap,
labeled Purple Mountains' Mountain's Majesty,
Crayola's Rosetta stone, a god gone corporate,
an international conspiracy to grab a child's soul.

But what I'd like to believe is that Yahweh
most mornings strolls though his garden toward a hillside
door, tugs it open, waves on light, revealing
countless casks holding dyes, glimmers, petals,

screams, crushed insects, explosions, rust,
ointments, folded galaxies, sage, giggles,
lightning streaks, old lady dandelion hair,
locomotives, wine, grief (some casks leak),

blank peacock feathers, neon gas, angel raiment rags.
Then, Yahweh plays.

Gracia Grindal

EVE REACHES FOR FORBIDDEN FRUIT

"Thou shalt not eat of the golden fruit of the tree
In the midst of the garden," the voice a negative
Of flesh drawn toward the deadly lust to live,
To know, to touch forbidden fruit, to see.
A tongue hisses, mocking the cruelty
Carved in commands only deities can give.
"Reach out, my lovely, toward the web I weave—"
His tongue glistens with possibilities.
A globe breaks like a glass of ruby wine
Filling the fissures of the earth with shade.
Knowing, I bid my languid lover dine.
We feed on chaos in the naked glade,
My appetite gorges on shady night.
The earth goes flat, the moon a plate of light.

EVE FACES HER GUILT

The garden flowering behind us, we fussed about
The reasons why, and how we were deceived:
How gullible I was, his gallantries,
The way the serpent tempted me to doubt,
The hard scrabble of work. My daily bouts
With tears watering the fragrant leaves
Left me garnering up the yellow sheaves,
Working the human consequences out.

Remembering Eden in each other's arms
We struggled for the paradise we lost.
Too soon the lure of knowledge lost its charm.
Driven together we joined our dust to dust,
Wedding our faults, making our peace again,
Lost in a world spinning beyond our ken.

THE TEMPTER RETURNS

He kept coming back, hissing in the trees
Whispering sly seductions, making me think
Life would be sweeter if I yielded to his pleas.
Adam grew dull, the children over the brink,
I was his first, he said, "Keep reaching out to take
Fruit flushed with ripeness, you are getting old."
Age drooped before me, remote and bleak,
I longed to taste it, once again be bold.
The little treaties that I made with him
Did nothing, ink spelling out sorrow, pain,
Betrayals to our flesh, hurt to the brim,
Leaving us spent and wasted, praying for rain
To wash away the grievous fault we shared,
The war we waged but never quite declared.

MARY NURSES JESUS

The let down, my milk coming in, the shepherds gone,
Music like silver impressed on the skies above
Here in this infant, the tempter's curse undone,

Divinity now lying in the rough—
A stable, the friendly beasts, our flesh like theirs.
Young as a bud, I pondered what this meant:
The baby in my arms, God unawares
Rooting around to find my virgin breast,
A wonder every newborn mother knows
Feeling his perfect form growing from me
Made in my image, fresh as a summer rose,
It happened in me, without me, stunned, I could see
How nature works through us, our carnal ways,
A permanence that stamps and spends our days.

MARY WATCHES HER SON ENTER JERUSALEM

Watching people flocking to hear him preach
Holding their limbs up to be touched and healed,
I pondered again the love I heard him teach,
Knowing his enemies wanted to kill
My son reverenced the heart, the very truths
They twisted to their own ends. Puzzled, amazed.
At all he knew, his purity of youth.
I saw him, following him that deadly day
He rode like David through the crowd, a king.
Hosanna they shouted, throwing their garments down.
My flesh made strange, I felt my body sing,
Palms now a green road as he swept into town
A Caesar, soon to hear his subjects cry—
My Lord, my own sweet child—be crucified.

Malcolm Guite

THE SIX DAYS WORLD TRANSPOSING IN AN HOUR

Twenty-four seven in "the six days world,"
In endless cycles of unnerving news,
Relentlessly our restless hurts are hurled
Through empty cyber-space. Is there no muse
To make of all that pain an elegy,
Or in those waves of white noise to discern
Christ's inner *cantus firmus*, that deep tone
That might give rise at last to harmony?

We may not seal it off or drown it out,
Nor close our hearts down in the hour of prayer,
But listening through dissonance and doubt,
Wait in the space between, until we hear
A change of key, a secret chord disclosed,
A kind of tune, and all the world transposed.

HOW TO SCAN A POET

My doctor tells me I will need a scan;
I tap a nervous rhythm with my feet,
"Just count to five," she says, "and then sit down.

The gist of it is printed on this sheet,
So read it over when you are at home.
We'll have a clearer picture when we meet."

I read the letter in a waiting room,
Its language strangely rich for one like me
Image, Contrast, Resonance; a poem

Slips into view amidst the litany
Of Latin terms that make our medicine
A new poetic terminology.

The door is opened. I am ushered in
To lisp my list of symptoms, to rehearse
The undiscovered art of naming pain.

"It's called *deep inspiration*," says the nurse,
"Draw deep for me then simply hold your breath
And stay composed." So I compose this verse.

She says, "We dye for contrast, to unearth
Each hidden image, which might bring
Some clue that takes us closer to the truth.

Be still and I will pass you through the ring,
Three passes, all in rhythm, and you're free,
The resonance will show us everything."

And now my Muse says much the same to me,
Scanning these lines, and calling me to sing.

AMEN

When will I ever learn to say *Amen,*
Really assent at last to anything?
For now my hesitations always bring
Some reservation in their trail, and then
Each reservation brings new hesitations;
All my intended *amens* just collapse
In an evasive mumble: *well, perhaps,*
Let me consider all the implications . . .

But you can read my heart, I hear you say:
For once be present to me, I am here,
Breathe in the perfect love that casts out fear
Open your heart and let your yea be yea.
Oh bring me to that brink, that moment when
I see your full-eyed love and say *Amen.*

A RONDEAU FOR LEONARD COHEN

Like David's psalm you named our pain,
And left us. But the songs remain
To search our wounds and bring us balm,
Till every song becomes a psalm,
And your restraint is our refrain;

Between the stained-glass and the stain,
The dark heart and the open vein,
Between the heart-storm and the harm,
Like David's psalm.

I see you by the windowpane,
Alive within your own domain,
The light is strong, the seas are calm,
You chant again the telling charm,
That names, and naming, heals our pain,
Like David's psalm.

A VILLANELLE FOR EASTER DAY

As though some heavy stone were rolled away,
You find an open door where all was closed,
Wide as an empty tomb on Easter Day.

Lost in your own dark wood, alone, astray,
You pause, as though some secret were disclosed,
As though some heavy stone were rolled away.

You glimpse the sky above you, wan and grey,
Wide through those shadowed branches interposed,
Wide as an empty tomb on Easter Day.

Perhaps there's light enough to find your way,
For now the tangled wood feels less enclosed,
As though some heavy stone were rolled away.

You lift your feet out of the miry clay
And seek the light in which you once reposed,
Wide as an empty tomb on Easter Day.

And then Love calls your name, you hear Him say:
The way is open, death has been deposed,
As though some heavy stone were rolled away,
And you are free at last on Easter Day.

Jeff Gundy

CONTEMPLATION AT THE BAR R RANCH

Both the owner and his daughter said we'd have to see the crosses,
so of course I tried to avoid them. But wandering aimlessly

after sublimity as I do on free afternoons, I followed a sign
that said "Baptismal" down a narrow way

and stepped carefully on rocks across the icy creek.
When I looked up, there they were, enormous,

big enough to crucify a pteranodon or a giraffe.
As I climbed the muddy path some part of me said,

I have to safeguard my doubts, and another remembered
how the old picker said to Goodman, *I find*

the prettiest woman in the room and play every song for her.
Too edgy to eat, Salinger's Franny tried to pray

the Jesus prayer all the way through homecoming.
With the sun low behind the crosses, I could barely look.

Thin grass, lichens, rocks, and gravel lay low all around,
stunned by some brutal devotion not their own.

Three weeks to solstice. Faint thin birdsong.
So many trees, so many rocks, so many women

whose lives and bodies I will never touch.
The creek rippled on, Shasta glowed in the chilly haze,

a strand of spider silk glinted in and out of sight.
Breathe in: *This is paradise.* Breathe out: *I must go.*

EVENING WITH LONG BOOKS

Each man is a half-open door
leading to a room for everyone.
—Tomas Tranströmer

My friends say Tolstoy really got into the heads of his female
    characters.
They give him credit. They talk dreamily of the books they love,

books so long only two will make a whole course. This seems to me
like making twelve gallons of chili and eating nothing else till it's gone,

but I smile and listen. My friends are smarter than me and more
    patient,
surely. I'm the only guy in the house tonight so I get my own room

with a good foam mattress, a bad desk, windows that open on other
    rooms.
I make up the bed and lie down with Tranströmer's poems, ten or
    twenty

lines on a page, fewer words in fifty years than Tolstoy or George Eliot
put down in a decent work week. *Every man is a half-open door.*

The door to my room is cracked open, lights blaze outside. My friends
are all upstairs. If I don't shut the light off, no one will. The wind

will settle toward morning, the waves begin again to spell their single
complicated word. Waiting for the ferry we watched a hawk

try to lift a four-foot snake from the shallows, drop it, circle, swoop
and grab again and lose its grip and veer away. Oh, how sweet would

that meat have been, how grand a feast, how we would have cracked
and sucked the bones, how long we could have made that story last.

Calm Sunday in Klaipeda

It was the holy part of the day, his loved ones asleep
in other countries, him with no duties and rooms

full of quiet. He ate his dark bread with brie and jam,
pressed out two cups of dark coffee. And that

must be the sun, skulking like a grown-up boy who knows
it's been too long since he visited his mother. He has

no excuse but all is forgiven, she will open the curtains,
haul up the shades, crack the windows though it's

far too cold for that. We will ring all the bells
in the quiet church across the street, unscrew

the doors from the jambs, dismantle all the borders,
forgive the Russians whether they like it or not.

And mercy will pour down like sunshine in the grand
photographs in the vast inscrutable book he bought

for ten euros at the bookstore downtown, a store
full of books translated out of the language he knows

so that he could read only the authors' names.
Truth must be personal, said Kierkegaard, home

from another of his long, brooding walks. And yet
not merely private. You *shall* love the neighbor,

he insisted. Outside the window the church is solid
and pale, three stories and a squat round tower,

in the tower three narrow windows that reveal
nothing. Winter sun warms the green roof,

but the entrance is still in shadow.

DETERMINISM ON A SUMMER MORNING IN THE MIDWEST

> *Ibn 'Ata' (d. 922) declared that [rida] is "the heart's
> regard for what God chose for the servant at the
> beginning of time, and it is abandoning displeasure."*
> —Bismillahir Rahmanir Rahim, "What Is Rida?"

1.
There's no such thing as free will and that's bad, or so says
Stephen Cave in *The Atlantic*. I guess that explains my decision

to read his whole grim article this morning, when I had plans
to walk around town, mail a package, buy a retirement card

for Susan, have a cup of coffee uptown as I always think
I should but rarely do. The problem, says Cave, isn't that

we don't *have* free will but that we need to think we do.
"It seems that when people stop believing they are free agents,

they stop seeing themselves as blameworthy for their actions."

2.
Dostoyevsky said, *If God is dead, everything is permitted,*
but the claim has not been proven to my satisfaction.

There are tulips and a daffodil on the table, in a glass
mostly full of water. There's a child's orange coat hanging

by the door. Who can say when the gates will open,
or what they'll reveal? Lisa's five or six tables away,

but her voice is the only one I can hear. Not the words,
just the tone. She passed along what sounds like bad news,

though not a catastrophe. What am I doing here?
Anywhere? It feels like I'm free, but only because

I have no idea what to do next. OK, I have several
ideas, just none that seem halfway interesting.

Out on the sidewalk a woman with a child's hand
clutched in hers passed one way, then back the other.

3.
Blonde on Blonde is fifty years old. Dylan is still touring.
There are songs that mean more to me than most

of the Bible. I have fair-sized chunks of the Bible
and dozens of Dylan songs "by heart," which means

"lodged in my brain, to emerge at unpredictable moments."
Should I leave them by your gate? Should I wait?

4.
I have to go pee or just go home. There's nobody at home,
nobody in my office, I'd be safe either place, it would

seem like I could do anything I wanted. Maybe not
disappear, or fly, or grow hair on the top of my head.

I could get in the car and drive straight north to the lake,
or cross the bridge to Canada, or take the small roads

across the open prairies till they dwindle into traces.

5.

MS Word fixes some of my typos, but not all of them.
People I know keep wandering along the sidewalk.

The woman I thought was Susie isn't. The sky
is gray but no rain yet. The spring has been miserable.

I pay young folks to mow, spread mulch, things I could do
but just don't want to. I get on the bike and tear around

the country roads instead, come home sweaty and pleased
with myself. The tomatoes are still in their little plastic pots.

The broccoli is leggy and sulking. Who wants to believe
it's all my fault? Who wants to believe it isn't?

6.

"Wherever you go, you take yourself with you,"
says Neil Gaiman, also "You can't make me love you."

I'm pretty sure that when he said you he didn't mean me.

7.

For years I've loved the notion of being lost,
thanks to Rebecca Solnit's *Field Guide to Getting Lost,*

not to mention Jesus and Thoreau. I've lived for decades
in the same house on the same street in the same town

but I've never quite gotten my head around being saved.
In an old poem I wrote something like "He decided to save

his soul, the way some people save / handkerchief boxes . . ."

8.

"Sleep," says Picard-as-Locutus. "He's exhausted,"
says Dr. Crusher. But he's telling them how to destroy

the Borg vessel before they assimilate everybody.
There are many ways to awaken. Some are fatal.

Others will save you, if you can be saved, whatever
it means to be saved. Data figures it out quickly

and the cube ship explodes, leaving the Federation
safe and the members of the Borg collective

in a spectacularly less structured condition.

9.

I still don't know how to be myself and belong
to something at the same time, much less rest easy

where I am, however pleasant, however graced.
These days all I want to do is sleep, and eat,

and ride my bike for hours on the sweaty blacktops,
drain my water in the first ten miles, fog my glasses,

not bother to glance at the corn to this side,
the soybeans to the other, slow as little as I dare

at the blind corners where a pickup may be
blazing my way with its oblivious tons of doom.

Charles Hughes

OUT OF THE DEPTHS

> *Agere contra.*
> —Ignatius of Loyola

God isn't love or isn't God. This is,
For doubt, its royal flush: God can't be both.
I'm caught up in the logic and the mood,
Hemmed in by facts, one fact, the world's abyss
Of suffering and injustice, how it's loath
To love: no God or else one far from good.

Pray, then, to learn love's work from Christ, to trust
The rumored beauty of this world renewed,
Which—like some long-lost heirloom tablecloth,
Once wedding gift, lace linen, still discussed—
Doesn't show up but should.

* * *

Agere contra is a Latin phrase meaning *act against*. It is an important concept of Ignatian spirituality, encouraging acting against one's natural inclinations in some times of spiritual desolation.

OCTOBER FRIDAY

A boy is walking home from junior high,
Happy because it's Friday and because
Pure sun is setting leaves on fire, although
He doesn't really see the reds and golds
Flaming along the way he always goes.
The radiance pulls him, and he feels its pull.
In minutes, he'll be home and changed and out,
Throwing around a football with a friend.
In Vietnam, the war is ramping up.
The boy hasn't yet heard of Vietnam,
Nor does he know that war is prophecy
And adamant, perpetual self-fulfillment.
He's been baptized and taught that God is love,
That Christ died for our sins and rose again
For our salvation—none of which he doubts
Or thinks about. He'll lean and stretch for a catch,
Running as if possessed, the cooling air
Washing against his face and reaching arms.
God doesn't stop the wars and maybe can't,
The world being powerful and God being love
(A thought a later self will come to think).
The boy, this afternoon, is bathed in firelight.
He'll grab the pass, crash an imagined goal line,
And go inside for supper and the night.
Outside, the leaves will lose their fire and dim.
A little breeze will blow up and begin
To take a few of them, then more and more,
And drift them down in whispers, which a witness,
Alert in the dark, could well hear as a calling—
To burn, as God-like leaves do in the fall.

"FEAR NOT, LITTLE FLOCK"
—*Luke 12:32*

This morning—outdoors, walking—
I count the birds I see:
Clouded late winter sunlight
Discloses only three—

Small, half a block behind me,
Ascending the mid-sky,
Diving, but upward, urgent—
As if to rise or die

In ecstasy, in answer
To what they are and know
Of seasonal transitions
That come too slow, too slow—

As if plummeting toward heaven
Might really hurry spring—
As if the times and seasons
Have been encouraging.

Who wouldn't turn to watch them
On hearing reckless cries
Above the traffic's clamor,
Perhaps even recognize,

As Christ-hued, the exertions
By three bird-specks of brown,
Etching on pale-lit grayness
That up can look like down?

NEW YEAR'S GEESE

El Niño winter. January. Geese
Fly high above this still suburban street,
So high I hear their cries, then have to strain
To see them—not a V—dark flecks of ink
Bunched on a gray construction paper sky.
They're indistinct, seemingly in distress,
Moving as bubbles move in boiling water,
And getting nowhere. Honking wildly, they
Appear to have encountered unawares
Some mortal and invisible enemy.
I can't help but admire their stamina.
Minutes go by. The geese keep grappling with
Whatever chaos holds them in its grip.
I'm thinking, *Who does better most days?*—when
Suddenly silence falls. For no clear reason,
The nonstop caterwauling stops. One second
And two and three . . . eternity . . . but brief:
A single voice takes up its chant-like call.
Others call back; and back and forth, the geese
Soon antiphon themselves into formation—
A fresh, clean V—in which they vanish. Me?
There can be mercy deep in memory,
I've found—unseen, piercing as parting sound.

WINTER BIRDS

"But what about the birds that don't fly south?"
A boy—age six?—arms full of books—is asking.
The library is closing. We're in line.
"Some birds don't mind the cold," a woman answers.
"They have warm nests. Their feathers keep them warm."
The boy hesitates, then rejoins, "But Grandma . . ."
He hesitates again as if he's gathered
His grandmother can't tell him any more.

Since Christmas, it's been bitter cold. Tonight
Will tumble icily down to zero or
Below, and there may be, there may well be,
Some birds close by that die tonight, some birds—
The youngest, oldest, hungriest—some birds
That, in this kind of cold, may well shrink deep
Into nests and feathers, just not deep enough
To keep them shivering until the morning.

The boy, his books checked out, his grandmother—
They're moving toward the door. She's promising
Hot chocolate and Christmas cookies once they're home.
Her voice trails off . . .
                            They've vanished now, although
Two common, everyday realities
Stay put and visible like winter birds:
The suffering and death of innocents;
Love's presence, unavailing, undeterred.

PRAYING FOR EYES TO SEE

"They say: 'These are useless sacrifices. These men will
perish, but the structure of life will remain the same.'
Even thus, I think, people spoke of the uselessness of
Christ's sacrifice and of the sacrifices of all the martyrs for
the sake of the truth."
—Leo Tolstoy

I've watched the surface of a lake being pitted
Implacably by the blunt blows of raindrops
And felt my heart sink,
Perhaps because the rain seemed never-ending,
Of how it so symmetrically kept pounding
Into that flat surface—
Which lay exposed, spread-eagle and defenseless—
Innumerable wounds, each one, on impact,
A tiny fountain.
My point is I forgot, in my distraction,
The living-dying-living, otherworldly,
Deep-hidden vista,
The gliding, darting, dark-lit, time-lapse beauty,
All flux and permanence together, balanced
Below, unbattered,
As if it were a work of art created
To mean God's mercy in the guise of matter,
As a remembrance—
So when I learn some latter martyr's story,
Lord, let me see beneath the final beating
And what he suffered,
His freezing cell, its brimming, spilling toilet,
The handcuffs, prison bed, bored guards unleashing

Their rubber truncheons—
Let me take in the why of his imprudent
Refusals to recant, try to imagine
The soul inside him.

Jean Janzen

HIVE

Honeybees hum in the chimney
as they work, nothing deterring
them from their devotion to our home,
not smoke, chemicals, or beekeepers.

Forty years of honey stored
inside the brick flue for generations
unknown, all of it perfectly
packed into tiny compartments,

much like our own gathering
and storing, what we guard like
worker bees fanning the queen.
In a dream the chimney overflows

in summer heat, honey streaming
over the roof. Time to sort, to give
and throw away, I say, tossing
books, clothes, even money.

And still I awaken into disbelief—
my unimaginable abandonment.
O sweet world, your mornings of lips
and birdsong. The deep sleep of winter.

THE COMEDY OF TABLE

Old Abram at the oaks of Mamre
squints into the noonday sun
and bids the travelers welcome.
Bread and a tender calf, and then
the promise of the impossible,
Sarah laughing in the kitchen.

After the baskets of bread crumbs
and fish bones, after the wounds
and the burial, the intimate supper
at Emmaus, his hands glowing

Rublev paints the Trinity
seated at a tilted table,
a goblet ready to slide off.
Open your hands and your mouth,
they sing, as the stars sail over me.

"TRAVEL LIGHT"

Command or description, I want
to glow as I walk through my day,

as I drift through the halls
of the nursing home where I find you

dozing in your bed. I want you
to see how I'm learning to float,

the air thinning between our kisses.
And yet, the weight—harvest of moon

and fruit heavy with sugar. In August
heat I lift a melon, smell this long

summer pressed against the earth,
what I will carry to you tomorrow.

THREE FOR THE BODY

1

All those sermons about the seductions
of the flesh. Spiritual life, the elders said.
But who could hear it without the intricate

cochlea and hammer, or the wondrous
muscles of lips and face to form the words?
I sat supported by a spine balancing

my head, heart muscle pulsing—home
for the mind, according to the Hebrews,
nest of bowels cradling my emotions.

2

In the Book of Kells the Incarnation
Initial swells with bodies, elaborate
swirls around humans and animals—

cats, rats, moths, and angels sharing
equal space. See the harmony, and how
the borders are pressed by fecundity,

how nothing is fixed, the top curve
of the Initial having burst open, fragrance
of lilies announcing the outpour.

3

Body as temple, the apostle declares.
All around, the courtyards of clamor,
our appetites and aches crowding the doors

while inside, the table shimmers.
I saw it first in my parents' faces
and in the glare of sunlit snow.

Beyond the striving and failures, the quiet
center waiting, curtains parted for entry,
the body's hunger to be known.

THE LAST WORD
after Frederick Buechner

And who is this young stripling beside you,
Uncle George bellows from his hospital bed
in Chicago, untamed city of wind and soot.
His white hair in a tousle, he sits up,
surveys us, this man who terrified me
as a child with his fiery preaching.

Young marrieds in the '50s, we stand beside
his rumpled bed above the traffic
on Michigan Avenue, sirens echoing.
In this city my husband is studying
the body's diseases while I read *Hamlet*
and *King Lear,* both of us seeking cures.

Lear cries "Howl, howl, howl!"
Surgeon enters with his sharpest knife,
pours medicine that kills before it heals.
No rescue without nakedness, Shakespeare writes,
Lear fumbling the button at Cordelia's throat,
all of us leaning into the final word, *mercy.*

Philip C. Kolin

CREATION

He peoples the darkness with stars:
Eyes in all that vastness.
He stores sunlight in his tabernacle
Meting out each day enough to gladden
The trees and moons with their changing
Colors. Vestments over land and sea.

Space is a trellis in his garden.
He scatters organelles, pods, bulbs,
Protozoa, spermatozoa, ovaries
All bursting into blossom. Every womb
Awaits the coronation of its birth.
Stone fruits and star apples.

FEATHERS
For Christina Moreland

Relics from the sky, she calls them
her box of feathers. Finds them
in the unlikeliest of places: in keyboards,
cupboards, closets, aisles, on sills
like soft-winged vespers when she pulls
the shades down at night. Sometimes
they're so small she can't tell
if it's a feather or a fossil of her hair.

But long, bold-shafted feathers, too,
sometimes fall before her gathering eyes:
quills on which saints inscribe visions
and declarations of dependence
on the Holy Spirit, which she bends
to fit into her cardboard chapel.

Picks them up on beach walks,
gifts the waves have sent her,
incarnate cries murmuring in the surf.
Recalled in the diary she keeps of feathers:
whirlwind, water, sun, molt, and fire.

Joy for the morning, this fowler's dark
that clasps the undercarriage of his light.

AUTUMNALS

Between retirement and bereavement
come autumnals, the gilded leaves
shekels in crisping-pins;
puffed up sparrows on outmost branches;
quests for surety.

But uncertainty is also a catechism—
our brief expanse
the willowy lights in late October
flickering, blurring day
from shadows descending.

But keep your reflections calm, see a pond
become an opalesque canvas
where fish create expanding circles,
their fins sleeking like angel wings,
a world yet to be.

JOB'S BLAZON

My skin sinks in sackcloth,
Worry canyons me with wrinkles.
Gaunt, cleft-hewn, I am a monument
To my defeated, dying self.

My voice from my pleas is
Asundered. They are buried
In the mortuary of the dark.

I stumble in the season of night
On a path of briars, biers, and thorns,
Pricking me into memory.

My body aches with time.
Every minute consumes endless seconds
As if I were a living cadaver
And the clock a hungry predator
Tearing my grey flesh from
My stale, lime-soaked bones.
My veins shrink
Like deflated balloons,
Full once, now airless rubble.

Once I loved the sea
Bathed in its giddy spray,
Tasted its salty liquor.
Today my tears burden
The waves overflowing with
My misery, with my misery.

UNCLE MOSES' DREAM

What if that brave Emmett
had somehow managed to escape,
my boy who had done all that talking,
a word or maybe two before those
thirsty fists demanding
to be quenched in his blood
slammed my door down looking for him.

Say he heard their pickup truck.
Say he jumped out the window
of my clapboard house and ran through row
after row of burly-cheeked cotton
until even the lily-white moon
could not follow him.

Say he made it to that line
of loblolly pines and hid
in the colored cemetery; no whites allowed
their children or their womenfolk to go there
where the haints of lynched men lurk,
hate messages singed into their chests.

Say he made for the river
seeking safety in the bulrushes,
the final resting place of so many slaves
who ran for freedom, hoping his battered
breath might last long enough under
the cesspooling water, stringy-fingered
weeds and copperheads
grabbing for his ankles.

Say the Tallahatchie had not turned
vengeful, angry that some black boy
would pollute the waters where white men
feed their families and their lusts.

Say, too, from the river he searched
for a ditch to lie in, coffining him
from the burlap-hooded vigilantes
swooping over the countryside.

Say a thunderstorm struck that night,
as they screamed to God
to let them catch the boy before
the lightning or the buzzards did.
Say, too, they scattered black
and white posters all over
Mississippi vowing to bury him.

Then say, just say, how he almost
found the train tracks which might have
led him out of the Delta,
out of Egypt, I called my son.

Sydney Lea

THROUGH A WINDOW

I read a poem each Sunday   Our pastor calls this *Ministry
of Verse*   I try to find a poem not just she but anyone
will get   A short poem if I can for fear someone like Timmy
who isn't all that into poems to begin with may complain

I try to select some lines that represent what I believe
and more or less what the people there believe   I have friends too
outside the church who cannot believe that I in fact believe
say in miracles   They ask can you really believe they're true

exactly   Poems cannot be exact   I'm thinking how I'll sound
My vanity lives on   I don't read my own poems which grow shorter
as I grow old   I once imagined I must go on and on
to get at things I thought I knew but I know more than ever

I know nothing now   No my friends I don't believe exactly
in miracles   I believe inexactly   I see Mary
Magdalene just for instance in that garden quite unclearly
Still I see her   I see Tess as well who's married to Timmy

and seems confused   Well she *is* confused   Dementia has her down
Her husband's there   He holds her hand   Timmy holds things together
I've thought at times like anybody I couldn't hold my own
yet I'm alive   I hear a bird sing   one small massive wonder

EYE ON THE SPARROW

Tiny, almost an anti-weight,
if it blew off my palm in the wind I might not even notice.
Dashing against the backporch glass,
the bird fell onto logs I'd stacked there, or rather heaped.
I loaded our wood more neatly out in the shed
but this jumble of lumber reminded me
my life lacked grace.

Wind didn't kill the bird but misprision.
My oldest daughter had just given birth to twins,
and I was thinking of them of course
when I saw the sparrow. Spring's a hopeful season.
I'd like to imagine new beginnings,
not ponder for instance the self-styled Christian crusaders
I heard about lately, devoted to killing police,

to launching Armageddon.
They claim these are days of Antichrist,
and I could almost agree—for other reasons.
Thou shalt not murder is among the Commandments,
I'd remind the crusaders,
all nine of whom live in Detroit,
a place near hell in abiding Depression.

Days are bad worldwide,
though in gospel God's eye takes in the smallest sparrow.
Vile hooligans among us storm
over once having had a president who was other than white.
We're all human, and none of us saved,
and—as the old Greek said—
it might have been best if we'd never been born.

And yet to imagine a world devoid of hope
is too easy and lazy, I decide.
Outside the promising odors fly in on the wind:
damp mulch, old ice, wet mud and sap.
The sugar-makers hope for a few more gallons,
I hope for a few more years, to be with the children.
I open the stove and sweep the bird in.

JUNIOR SCHOLAR
*Truly I tell you, whatever you did for one of
the least of these, you did for me.*
—Matt. 25:40–45

The assistant professor suspends his reading
of a hyper-theoretical screed. He stares, off-handed,
at the trash-strewn alley below. An undignified view.
It's among the galling wages, he knows,
of his modest station, but he trusts in this volume and others like it:

he'll be moving upward. The author's urgent concern
is his nation's unjust social arrangements.
Our professor also feels for the dispossessed. He's read
on the subject—widely. Fall gloom pervades the alley,
but he sees a reeling wino within it,

at the cul-de-sac's deepest recess, far from whatever light
there may be. Not much. In fact, it's so dim that a rat,
as if it were night, patrols the wall
the derelict leans against. The rodent is only an arm's length
from the mumbling bum, who swivels a screw-off cap,

then lifts the jug to his untoothed mouth.
The professor finds small intrigue in such a tawdry mess
as the one below him. He has greater issues in mind,
above all the work he'll have to do
in order to climb from his own degrading tawdriness.

His wife will comply: no children for now, if ever.
He must return to the difficult book.
Though its tumble of seeming runes is a labor at best to decipher,
if this is the argot he needs, he'll cultivate it.
He eyes a Waterford flask in a nook,

half-full of barely affordable sherry. He's halfway tempted,
but a man had better think about his future.
He envisions himself as a rocket streaking
up through the ranks: one day he'll be envied by colleagues. He dreams
of fellowships, even festschrifts, not mere tenure,

no condescension to *him* again!
He looks down on the wretched drunk, who's flopped
    unconscious under
a shivering heap of indescribable fabric,
bits of cloth he has somehow assembled.
By now the light in the alley has gotten even dimmer,

and his view therefore has become more than ever uncertain.
Is that the profile of the rat he detects?
Some creature anyhow; it sniffs the covers, then climbs.
Might the foul thing actually bite into human flesh?
Who'd know? Our scholar returns to the text.

SHABBOS GOY

The early palaver of nestling crows
Outside my window in the white pine tree
Calls back a childhood in which such ruckus
Seemed prelude to possibility.

But I need to resist any rosy nostalgia:
I had my small troubles. I scarcely believed
The world would be nothing but pleasure and promise.
Even young, I wasn't entirely naïve.

Still I woke eager for my gang of pals,
For games we devised by improvisation,
And of course the vigor of our *own* palaver,
Which was graced by savvy. Or so we imagined.

A beloved friend from San Francisco,
Raised a Jew near Coney Island,
Now a *cultural Jew*, left here today.
I cherished the weeklong visit with him.

Our talk would get silly, but not truly childish.
It didn't involve emphatic insistence
On one team's being superior
To some other, to mention a tiny instance,

Or on faith, for much larger. For near sixty years,
There've been very few secrets we haven't shared,
However wildly different our backgrounds,
With this man I love. So I wonder from where

I get the sense we left some things
Unsaid, and I wonder what they might be?
In this after-time, it's as if I were thirsty.
This is not, to be sure, confined to me

In my dealings with that particular man.
It's just that his stay has roiled a thought:
The older I get, the less I suspect
I'll *ever* get my ardors across—

To God, to the woman I'll love until death,
To our burgeoned family, to other dear friends—
If I can't identify them myself.
Though spring days grow long, some dusk descends

On my soul sometimes, and not only toward dark.
No need to acknowledge it's metaphorical.
Whatever its nature, I proceed through that darkness
Like a Shabbos *goy.* Such as I'm able,

I spread light, although I fear it's feckless.
Talk! Talk! Talk! the nestlings gabble.

Karen An-Hwei Lee

THE GOOD DAY

After the bad day, I pray for good days
in the world. On good days, women
are safe, brushing out their hair
while waiting for God to say hello.

The world is an unwalled garden
of fruit we enjoy without worrying
about fork-tongued, talking serpents
lying. We taste and see life is good.

On good days, we walk on the paths
to the rivers. We are never catcalled
or spat upon, never ordered to leave
while gazing at stars or figs, pears,

satsuma oranges or mangosteens,
never questioned about our origins.
We are never eclipsed by our fears
of violence personified in the night.

We are fully human and fully iron
at the same time. This is God's blood,
goodness poured out like first aid
for a blighted, burning world. Days

are so good, they taste like lychees.
Family names and faces are loved.
We drink goodness and swim in it,
bathe in it, born in the good days.

Our churches are churches, the brides
of Christ, not sites of carnage.
During the good days, I peel and eat
a ripe pomegranate in the garden

without hesitation, free of the grip
of underground assassins taking us
from our mothers, trapping us
in cavernous, endless winters—

without pondering if this seed
I swallow is my last if a bullet
will meet my flesh and bone
as I walk out the front door.

SONGS OF COMFORT

The friendly cellist with a big heart, a long-time resident
of a neighboring town where I grew up, who received
bouquets from the flower shop where I trimmed roses,
said his favorite thing to do after returning from a trip
was grocery shopping, savoring the essentials of small life
away from the airports and applause: buying milk, fruit
like blessings of solace: bread, tea, local honey in a jar
slow, lovely as sarabandes, those songs without words
aired in isolation through the pandemic. After his dose,
Yo-Yo Ma plays an impromptu concert for others waiting
in the fifteen-minute interval after the shots to monitor
allergic reactions. Masked, he lifts his cello out of its case,
perhaps his favorite one named Petunia, then tightens

the horsehair bow adroitly. The cello, with its mellow
notes of melancholy mingled with hope, fills the hall,
like the light at the end of the tunnel, the residents say.
Light at the end of the tunnel. I know it must be true
because I would never put this trite sentence in a poem
otherwise. God is waiting for us to pay attention:
God is waiting in the light.

IN PRAISE OF SMALL LIVING

I do not mind small living. I love the minuteness—
ducks and geese grooming, swans preening lazily,
sharing our rice and beans, spending hours indoors
with lungfuls of room air, going outside for a walk
after the rain. I can suffer wearing a mask, in fact,
prefer it in cold weather with no need for lipstick.
I hold an umbrella by its bamboo handle, just so.
I enjoy the smallness of this life. I love the edges
of souls looking at other faces on a screen, praying
about who and when, and where we are going.
There is a way to savor the small in this pandemic—
a sad consequence of being so numerous on earth.
Let us focus on the essentials if only for ten minutes
before jumping into the next glass puddle of hours,
each breath marking the tender schism of life
against death. The wind stirs up dust in the night
when crocuses bloom under snows, and the world
opens again with gusts of saffron, blustery splendor—
a year has fled and the wind agitates heat and rot,

the yard soon fragrant with roots of growing things.
It roars up in the trees like midnight surf pounding
when you walk on the coast, a broken moon in chords
of light on the waves, glossy, rolling back and back—
dogs do not bark, the wild doves hold their coos,
neighbors box up their tossed shell wind chimes—
the wind, a formless cleansing, is only the motion
mingled with a commuter train floating over rails
in the midnight rhythms of rest and reassurance.

DEAR MILLENNIUM, ON QUARANTINE DREAMS

As I wake in the morning, facing the risk
of viral air wafting in open spaces

such as the market, a gas station, or dog park,
I dare to linger at the rows of fat peaches,

in no haste to choose one with a gloved
finger, a paper mask filtering the aroma

of ripening fruit palmed in my right hand.
The daily hours slow to the rate of dough

rising in an oiled bowl, the floured wood
petitioning silently for another round

of dimpling and kneading, for sweet rolls
instead of sourdough. Praying for loved ones

at a distance by making bread, I sugar the yeast
of kindred spirits with pleasure. In my dreams,

the loaves of bread fly all over the globe
like satellites radioing the old solace of toast,

the fierce reassurance of butterflies winging
south for winter in the mountains, their wings

fiery and crisp as buttered rye, oblivious
to the violence inflicted by an invisible

coronavirus wreaking havoc on civilization,
a virus so small, it is barely even a living thing.

PRAYER IN A CLOUD OF GINGER TEA

With a prayer, I lower my face in a cloud of ginger tea,
inhaling the promise of its sinus-clearing, herbal fire.

I'm learning the names of trees in this quiet township
past those days of girlhood greenery drifting sideways,

maple, elm, oak, cottonwood, then the nameless ones
autumnal, where the weight of all things sway together

to savor a moment of peace. In a crisis, let us be still
in the presence of sweet revelation, of the blessed

fragments of creation, for new voices tender as plums,
for psalms written in tongues other than our own

migrating to this place as a refuge even in this season,
for face coverings and the brassy, clean spice of roots

dug out of the earth, dutifully washed with our hands,
sliced and boiled for tea to cleanse the palate of salt,

a healing salve for the soul with its million crises.
I've said nothing about the illness of the universe

ravaging the soul and the body, nor the loneliness
plaguing the days of sheltering in place, the ache

of quarantine and solo lockdown, yet in this cloud
of ginger steam, I am made whole by the promise

of God's breath as a heavenly balm against hunger,
an unseen harvest festival bereft of a noisy crowd,

its fierce absence as a famine of human feeling.
We aspire to virus-free air with doses of mercy

so the long shadow of illness may lighten soon.
The twin blessings of our health and families

are spoons holding an ounce of uncooked rice,
a girl's handmade maraca tossed high in a tree—

a prayer yet to be answered, swaying in the arms
of Jesus who traces everything while silence rises

with the fall moon, a faithful musical instrument
unshaken in syncopation to the winds of change.

Marjorie Maddox

LOT'S DAUGHTERS
—*Genesis Ch. 19*

I.

At first—a leering mob circling
the house, jeering, dancing naked,
taunting the guests with their sex—
the daughters thought their father brave
to step outside, lock the door behind him,
stretch his arms out in protection.

But then, even he offered them up,
a sacrifice to protect strangers,
their father, the only
"righteous man" in a city destined for flames,
"Do with them what you like.
But don't do anything to these men."

Then their eyes were like Isaac's
below the knife,
the ram not yet in the bush,
the blade gleaming.

II.

What dread dug in the daughters'
betrayed hearts before the rioters—
struck blind—stumbled and fell,
unable to find the door,
Lot tugged back safely to the house?

Eyes straight toward Zoar,
did they hear their mother turning,
nostalgia sliced mid-sentence?
That life left behind,
what fixed their gaze away
from home—their father's almost-sacrifice,
or the intervention?

III.
No mention of mourning.
Their mother's unbelief behind them.
Too many miles.
The sun hot as horror.

IV.
When they fled to the cave
with no hope for heirs,
ashen cities behind them,
mercy was an unremembered flame.

This time, they sacrificed themselves,
holding out wine, lifting their dresses
to lure their father.
He twirled a drunken dance,
love or revenge spinning,
blurring vision.

"Rewarded" with sons,
they named them *From Father*
and *Son of My People*,
sang lullabies of fear and fire,
of what it means to wander,
to exile yourself,
to dream of salt and sand.

ESAU'S LAMENT

Without your words   my breath cracks
     dust on sand   without your words
my limbs break.   bones on graves
Oh my father   me too   without
    Can even this be stolen?   your words
No syllables of blessing left?
     No mouthed morsel of hope?   Oh my father
I alone am the hunted.   your words
    trapped and slain   me too
the spoils stolen again   me too
     that fair enemy
       without without

PRODIGAL BIPOLAR

Rebellion's a ribbon to wear in her bright, black hair
while she dances the jig with the neighbor's squealing pigs
and three convict sons. No one ever shakes a head and says,
"Girls will be girls." Not one. Not to the fretting parents who wring
their own necks in worry, who sing their own dirge to the sound
of strokes and stress. Not to the twirling deserter. Sex, the great
distinguisher, the great bearer of expectations, the great deceiver of grief
also confesses, "A child will be a child," but even here finds no relief
in equality, the agreed-upon diagnoses trampled in the mud
of some faraway farm while they wait, bruised ears to the ground,
for resounding footsteps that do not come, and do not come again,
the oxen rotted on the spit, the spoiled and rancid stinking up their now-
mortgaged estate in its own slaughtered, gender-neutral, bloody-bad way.

CATHETERIZATION

Start with the thin wisp
of hope some stranger hocked
in a hospital room while you waited—
heart pressed to chest—for your father
to die. Breathe in. Decades have skipped
to this beat with someone else dipping hope's
thread into the tiny creek at your wrist,
your fear swimming upstream to the damaged
cavern you inherited. Breathe out. *Papa, I hear*
your rhythm, the hum of deceptive rest,
the steady syllables of persistence.
What will hope find with its tiny eye,
with its very large memory of death?

Warren L. Molton

IF GOD IS MOSTLY PARADOX

If God is mostly paradox
    so that things contrary to common sense
    seem suddenly truth revealed
    and some unappealing sight
    is clearly *Imago Dei*, devilishly alight
    as though lit within at core
    by the very darkness we abhor
    and symbols of my soul's best hope are cast
    as models of betrayal, despair and death:
    Eve's fruit tasted then offered to Adam
    becomes Mary's Gift
    hanging as First Fruit
    of a new covenant of pardon,
    and the abandoned Garden
    because of Him
    becomes the New Jerusalem;
Then,
    let that mind be also in me,
    the one that takes in my off-stage acts,
    you know,
    those walk-the-talk naked facts,
    even my sneaky judas-pacts
    and transforms them all
    into something nothing short of new,
    like being born,
    like out of any godforsaken Friday
    Eastermorn.

GUY NEXT TO ME ON THE PLANE

He said he was a fallen catholic, lower case, and smiled.
Said he didn't intend to be, often pretended not to be,
but was. Said that God for him was like the guy next door,
a retired cop who packed a .38 and a billy club wherever
he went, but was nice as Hell. Insisted that the only Jesus
he ever really knew was his best bud, who lived across
the street, and on the other side lived the Holy Spirit,
a loving little old lady of ninety who made the best
sweet potato pie with toasted meringue he ever tasted.

He talked sort of sideways to me with his fingers laced
and his elbows braced on both arm rests, chin on his hands.
When I asked if he ever prayed, he dropped his hands
into his lap as though startled or just caught, and turning
toward me, he said, All the time anymore, since I had to
put down my tired and sick old dog, Sam. I took him
to the vet to do it. Laying there on the table with his great
head cupped in my hands, he looked at me with the most
loving and forgiving eyes I ever saw, like he was human
and I was his God, or something.

REQUIEM

When the rattler bit Tom, our great mule
whinnied in terror and his legs began shaking
into a death dance as he fought going down
and my big brother Ronnie and I slid off his
back, and he killed the snake. We had ridden
Tom down to our back forty to pick a gunny
sack of fresh green corn at our acreage
on the Carolina side of the Savannah River.

Finally Tom was on the ground and let me
stroke his neck as I waited in a death watch
while Ronnie walked the mile to our house
and Tom was still having spasms when he
returned with our hired man, two shovels
and a small pistol. When he pointed the gun
at Tom's brow, I turned away and jumped
as he fired; then the men began digging
at the near edge of the field.

Back at home, Ronnie nailed the snake through
its battered head to our beech tree in the back
yard, then using a sharp blade, he carefully cut
a red necklace around the snake's neck
and with mouse-nose pliers, peeled off its skin.
After a good scrubbing and a day in the sun
the skin was dry enough for him to begin rubbing
and working it with cotton seed oil until it was
soft and pliable, so he could slide it onto his belt
and wear it off to war in the South Pacific; but I
could never climb that bloodied beech again.

WHERE WILL YOU BE, GOD?

> *How oft when men have been at the point*
> *of death have they been merry! which their*
> *keepers call a lightning before death.*
> —*"Romeo and Juliet" Act 5, Sc. 3*

Where will you be, God,
    when life-time warranties are running out,
    familiar faces muddling and fading,
    lovers' own language sliding into recitation;
    and when I am wanting to rally
    to welcome one last poem,
    I keep colliding with that ancient passion
    for sacred sleep?
Where will you be, God,
    during kisses I can't return
    but only savor forever,
    when precious hands as though my own
    are touching for the last time
    my body's prayer places?
Where, God, will you be as my odyssey ends—
    this one that keeps folding
    back upon itself as though to start anew,
    this odyssey now running out of road?
Will you be so much me that I could miss you,
    so present that I am at last fully realized,
    or so far away that I am left
    with the nevertheless of mere surrender
    and my own bright laughter?

"HE DESCENDED INTO HELL"

This unlikely tomb
this once plundered vault
this meager poke of broken power
this moldy hole at the foothills
of Zion and the soul
this piddling down to fissure and fault
this dry womb
delivered us the earth angel
Jes-us
just like us
only wanting out more than in
yet staying there long enough
to cup one last beatitude
for those in ruin
and touch the tongues of hell's angels
on his way here.

Julie L. Moore

WHEN THE RAIN CLEARS

Standing on the street
in the early morning of late autumn,

I marvel to see, to my left,
over my own backyard, rain

and to my right, over my neighbor's barn,
only clear, dry air.

As I walk this line
drawn by the ordinary length of asphalt,

I think of the theologian who said,
God is on the loose now,

no longer hidden behind
the parochet, waiting for the high priest

to ask for the atonement
of his people's sins.

The rain has to clear somewhere.
Why not here? Like the road has rent

a veil that cloaks the fullness
of sight, separates shade from light.

MAILBOX

Rivers of Ohio rain cascaded
    into March, flooding streams & roads,
        then turned, one evening,

into snow, despite the 36 degrees
    & the way the groundhog,
        one month before, had missed his shadow.

So bending by the road,
    I picked up my mailbox
        knocked down once again

by snow swept into it, the plow's force
    strong enough to push
        a person over, but not really

massive, the favorite word
    that morning as the media described
        the 9.0 quake in Japan, the ensuing

tsunami. The axis of the whole world
    shifted several inches, they told us,
        shortening the day by 1.8 microseconds,

unlike Joshua's lingering sun.
    No horns signaled heroic victory.
        No moon refused to rise.

The dark storm of radiation
    loomed above like a god gone awry,
        while some kneeled in water, or snow,

begging for a word of explanation.

FULL FLOWER MOON
—for all the women at Safe Harbor House

The moon tonight smells like linen,
clean & pressed, spreading
its blue fabric over not just May's fields

but the willow by the pond,
the hens in the one-window coop,
the dog on the lawn,

poking her nose into the myrtle.
The sky tastes like a mug of tea,
warm & smooth with cream,

served at a welcoming table.
Should God suddenly speak,
the phlox would not be flummoxed

or the red-tailed fox baffled.
After all, green already
pulses through everything,

its rhythm in sync with this full
flower moon & the worm
below, writing a new word in dirt.

Would it really be so strange
if the still, small voice broke open
like a bulb beneath the earth,

then aired something sensible
as the strong stem lifting high
its lit lantern, signaling us

to join in, do what we were made to do?

COMPLINE
—*St. Meinrad Archabbey*

Forgive me my faults, my faults, my grievous faults,
she recites with the Benedictines preparing
for evening's darkening shroud—

her husband's figure standing erect
in her memory, his finger pointing at her,
threatening her, his once-sure vows

now dead, their hazy specters
prowling the hallways of her heart,
their long fingernails raking its walls.

While she chants—words, just words,
& barely sung—the Lord's Prayer
stumbles onto her tongue: *forgive us our trespasses,*

as we forgive those who trespass against us.
Not even an hour, nor is it sweet,
this prayer that arrests her,

exorcising the ghosts of promises past,
their furious, furious haunting.

THE PHILOSOPHER AND THE POET TALK
ON THE LAST WARM DAY IN FALL
—for Steve Broidy

My neighbor scrapes old paint
from the fence around his pasture,
an annual chore he attends to,
for he knows the white he applies
preserves each board.
I think of his recent essay,
peeling back the layers, as he said,
of online education, revealing a barren base
devoid of the body's subtle

gestures—
        how a screen cannot replicate
confusion written on a brow,
engagement flashing in the eyes,
or a hand touching a shoulder.
How a cursor cannot translate
the voice's inflections, nuanced
as the nod of his head, greeting me,
while he lays
        down his tool to rub my dog's ears,
while he motions toward the remaining wood,
tells how he'll finish the job before winter.

WHAT WE HEARD ON CHRISTMAS DAY
—with a line from Longfellow

Silence like early morning, like indigo
deepening at the bottom of the sea.
For hundreds of years.

No voice to say *this is the way.*
Or tomorrow, he comes. They raised
their questions, rose each morning, found

no answers. Unless you count
Wait. But after the hush
of prophecy, the long line of law,

exile centuries ago just a bitter aftertaste
in their empty mouths, sting
of dust on their ribs dulled, almost imperceptible,

a baby wailed. And if you listened close,
you knew your ears did not deceive you.
He had entered the ebony tomb

of Earth, loosening at last his long-held tongue,
the star a halo of song blaring overhead,
God is not dead, nor doth He sleep.

Angela Alaimo O'Donnell

FLANNERY'S DONKEY

> *"Ernest did the honors for the burros this Christmas pageant.*
> *He did all right at the Methodist dress rehearsal but when*
> *the big moment came and the church full of Methodists, he*
> *wouldn't put his foot inside the door."*
> —Flannery O'Connor

My mama's donkey *would be* a Catholic.
In this house there's no other way to be.
Braying his rosary on his rote rounds,
chawing his consecrated hay,
standing steady beneath the baptizing rain.
If ever there was a holy burro
Ernest is it. The Methodists see
only an ordinary donkey,
dumb creature, four hooves on the ground,
happy as a pig at a potluck
to preside at their Protestant play.
We shoulda known he would say *no*.
Our Catholic ass just could not feign
nor hide his scrupulous disdain.

FLANNERY & ESCHATOLOGY

*A truck driver driving up with a load of hay found a peacock
turning before him in the middle of the road, shouted,
"Get a load of that bastard!" and braked his truck to a
shattering halt.*
—Flannery O'Connor, "The King of the Birds"

It'll be like that, the Second Coming.

Making your way, laden with hay,

down the same old local road,

and there you are, stopped dead by Christ

with no idea what to say

in the face of such transforming

glory. Helpless without a code

to die by, tact is sacrificed

and candor coughs up the words we need.

He *was* a bastard, truth be told,

His father being not of this world

but the hidden one we just can't see

until a blue-plumed vision stalls your truck

leaving you blind and wonderstruck.

ST. LAZARUS

He knit him self up, a cable-stitch of skin.
Pushed his left eye in its socket, then his right.
Cracked the knuckles in his fingers (now so thin!).
Raised him self from the dirt and stood up right.

Lazarus, Lazarus, don't get dizzy.
Lazarus, Lazarus, now get busy.

Mary's weeping, Martha's made a cake,
Jesus is calling at the graveyard gate.
Your closest cousin, happy you are dead,
Eyes Martha's sheep and Mary's empty bed.

The chorus of voices sings him awake.
Once a body's broken, it cannot break.
He licks his lips and wags his muscled tongue.
Flexes each foot till the warm blood comes.
Turns from the darkness and moves toward the sun.
A step. A shamble. A dead-out run.

"AND THE ANGEL LEFT HER"
—Luke 1:38

So there she stood alone amid a stillness
as loud as any earthquake she had heard,
the eaves creaking in the absence of wind,
the hiss and tick of radiators warming
the house along with a soon-coming sun.
Her hands touch her belly, swelling already
like dough cupped close in an earthen bowl.
She knows it won't be long before she shows.
What to do with all this sudden silence?
Phone her boyfriend: *Joseph, I have news!*
Text St. Anne: *Dear Mother, I'm afraid.*
Drop to her knees, now weak with recognition
and kiss the space he filled a moment past
in answer to the question he had asked?

MAGDALENE'S MISTAKE
*"They have taken away my lord . . .
and I don't know where they have put him."*
—John 20:13

She knew these things: a body doesn't walk.
Soldiers can't be trusted. Gossips will talk.

She made her way there in the early dark.
She knew the stories—Noah and the Ark,

Jonah and the whale, David and the stone,
the things a man can accomplish alone.

Even so, she couldn't quite conceive
how a dead god could just up and leave

his beloveds behind, stricken with grief.
The empty days and nights, however brief,

reminding them of what they'd left behind—
death without rising for all of their kind.

She watched day dawn. Saw the budged rock.
Wept for all the bodies that would never walk.

FOR SHADOWMENT: VILLANELLE FOR THE SOLSTICE

Here, here in the crook of the year,
the crux and fix and flux of the year
light falls long across and dear.

Here in the ruck and dreck of the year
I glean and gather grace and gear,
here, here in the crook of the year.

Here is the neckbone of the year,
its knuckle sharp, its blade sheer,
where light falls long across and dear.

Hear the matins of the year,
the chant of praise and marrow fear,
here, here in the crook of the year.

Cheer the vespers of the year,
the prayers that rise from tongue to ear
as light falls long across and dear.

Clear your mind as night draws near.
Stead your heart and shed no tear,
here, here in the crook of the year
while light falls long across and dear.

THE STILL PILGRIM MAKES DINNER

It's Mother's Day and I have no mother.
She left and took my daughterhood.
It's hard to lose us both, recover.
A double grief. A day to brood.

I dredge the chops. Fry them in oil.
I slice the onion, wet as tears.
I wear my sackcloth apron, soiled
by meals I've made for thirty years.

For ashes, flour upon my head.
For prayers, the rise of scented smoke.
My mother, who is five years dead
lives in this meat, these eggs I broke,
this dish she taught me how to make,
this wine I drink, this bread I break.

Steven Peterson

FALLING

It wasn't nice,
No, wasn't nice,
To be called in the Garden by God.
He called us once,
He called us twice.
Was no answer a thing He thought odd?

He must have known,
We were His own,
He presumably knew what we did.
Or was He stunned
By what we'd done?
We refusedly shut up and hid.

That's us inside,
We hide, we hide,
As He's calling our names in the dusk.
And though we all
Regret the Fall,
To be falling is thrilling to us.

BOOMERANG

What I throw out to those I love
    Returns unreached to me, to me.
Bow stubborn knees to God above?
    I do if prayer turns round to me.

Slow whirling in an empty sky,
    Whoosh whooshing almost soundlessly,
Sole focus of my ear and eye,
    It all comes back to me, to me.

Yet selfless love I've read about
    And once or twice I've even known.
A miracle, as it turns out:
    Him swapped out for my blood and bone.

Of grace I have the hope for some
    And harken for that final bang.
O almost-soundless Savior come
    And break in two my boomerang.

SINGAPORE MEN'S BIBLE STUDY

We take our shoes off, leave them by the door,
And sit in batik shirts and khaki shorts
In Paul's colonial house in Singapore.

These bungalows, called "black and whites"—the sorts
In travel ads: black timbered, whitewashed walled—
Raise ghosts of Empire dealing imports/exports.

Tonight we expat businessmen sit sprawled
In wicker chairs along Paul's wicker bar
Because a Bible verse left us appalled.

It's this: "Tomorrow you will travel far
To buy and sell and count your business gains
But soon you'll vanish like a falling star."

Outside Paul's house the pelting tropic rains
Return to bring the heavy jungle scent
Of flowers rotting down to their remains

Repeating, with our beers, what that verse meant.

ADVENT

Around December first, the summer people
All have gone. Some had stayed to see the fall
And some for hunting season—all have gone.

We walk deserted roads. The first snows came
But dried away to traces in the ditch
And snowy patches on the forest floor.

In town the Christmas lights are blinking bright,
The tourists few. The locals seem subdued,
At peace with what some still call Advent time.

It's dark by four. We light a fireplace fire.
We have a drink and share a meal and read
Until it's time to go to early bed.

Outdoors to fetch tomorrow's wood, I stand
Beneath the stars. It's moonless, clear and cold.
The constellations reach like outspread hands.

Star bright but not at all a silent night,
There seems to be a constant trembling—
Someone surely there, someone almost here.

STOREFRONT THEATRE

Chicago. January. Present time.
"The core of winter," says our weatherman,
Whose forecast draws more eyes than local crime
Or something happening in Somewheristan.
A storefront theatre. A wind-chilled night.
We're in a tiny lobby, parka-packed.
A call: "The house is open!" Polite,
We set out folding chairs from where they're stacked.
Lights down. Lights up. Two actors: He and She.
Her voice. Then his. They whisper; we're that near.
Who now recalls the winter? Nobody.
We're anywhere. It's anytime. For here,
Between that simple stage and every seat,
A kind of cold communion turns to heat.

GHOST LIGHT

We've closed our theatres—a silence rules.
Homebound with Internet and iPhones, stocked
with everything we'd want as hoarding fools,
we double check to see our doors are locked.

Elizabethans closed their theatres
in plague years; Shakespeare scribbled poems for praises.
Today each playwright (one is me) utters
in keyboard clacks: free verse or formal phrases.

Yet theatres keep one bare light bulb burning
on stage, illuminating emptiness.
Tradition calls it a "ghost light," discerning
substance from shadows—like our faithfulness.

Let's ask the ghost light of our soul: Explain
this wait for life, or death, or deathless gain.

Yehiel E. Poupko

PICNICS

I remember my mother's room
and the windows overlooking the river
and the steel mills of my Pittsburgh childhood,
Bessemer furnaces stoked with coke and coal
and iron ore, boats and barges floating up
and down the river.

Yeshiva school children took day trips
to white hot molten rivers ladled into casts.
Pittsburgh is big shouldered we were told
and innocently thought this the original
while picnicking lunches on benches
by the river in the glow of iron coke and coal.

And now the mills and furnaces are empty,
orange rusty and skeletal against the green
wooded mountains that fall into the river
on whose banks is the room the nurse enters
with bottles and bags and needles and tubes
and pumps filled with molten pouring
into my mother who lies in the bed in the room
whose windows look out on the river
and its skeletons.

Once a month we picnic for lunch,
Blessed are You Lord our God
Who in His goodness nourishes the world . . .

in the room by the window on the green wooded
banks of the river our monthly chemo picnic
on the bank by the river, my mother's bed
shadowing the mills.

SO JOB DIED OLD AND FULL OF DAYS

Crammed and jammed
Bursting with days
Job died old and full of days

So full of days
He died
Died from days clotted with friends,
Eliphaz, Bildad and
Zophar
And don't forget Elihu
Late but stuffed with wisdom too
Friends certain and smug
Wiseacres knowing all
Everything about this life
Except of course the life of Job

So full of days
He died
Died from days God awed
The heavenly court and Satan dialogue
Travel reports and near endless silence
Lordly Master, God knowing all
Everything about the creation
Except of course the children of Job

So full of days
He died
Died from days teeming with nature
Treasury of snow, hems of oceans
The Venus hind birthing at dawn
The morning stars singing
Nature indifferent knowing all
Everything about the world
Except of course the emptiness of Job

Who died old and full of days

FROM SINAI

In the beginning
It was passed on
It all began when
It was passed on
Handed down
From lip to ear
Mind to heart
Not taught
Not instructed
Not told
Not given
And surely not discussed
It was passed on to us.
Ere we were
It was
It was passed on to us

And we became
The light
And the law
His flesh
In this life
Born again
Over and over
After each
And after every
No matter the fire
Restoration
The ways of holiness.
Eat not what they eat
Lie not with them and theirs
Clothe not thyself as they do
Speak not their tongues
Be that living passed on Torah.
Undone erased
You passed it back
In the ovens.

THE WORD BECOME ASH

For a while
We lived by the word
I am
You saw no image
I am
The word
Unseen and heard
Never to become flesh

All the seas ink
All the heavens parchment
Each blade of grass a quill
Each Jew a Scribe

We died by the word
Before the deed
Was done
The word became flesh
And the flesh became ash
We died by the word
Just one word
I am
Jude

SUFFER THE LITTLE CHILDREN . . .

To the ghettoes
Warsaw, Vilne, Lodz, Lublin
Then little children were brought to Jesus
Sara, Rebecca, Leah, Rachel
for him to place his hands on them and pray for them
Avraham, Yitzhak, Yaakov, Yosef
But the disciples rebuked those who brought them.
Miriam, Yocheved, Tzipora, Elisheva
Jesus said, "Let the little
Baraks, Gideons, Shimshons, Shmuels
children come to me,
Yissachars, Zevulons, Gads, Ashers
and do not hinder them,

Tirzas, Batshevas, Hannahs, Peninas
for the kingdom of heaven
Auschwitz, Treblinka, Majdanek, Sobibor
belongs to such as these."
Shlomos, Hizkiyahus, Yishayahus, Yirmiyahus
When he had placed his hands on them,
Yentls, Soshas, Mindeles, Shprintzas
he went on from there.
Belzec, Chelmno, Plaszow, Buchenwald.
And the little children came . . .

BEGINNING WITH THE CRUCIFIXION

and we
thought,
alright
he's only
one Jew
let them
have their
just one Jew,
appetite satisfied
with just
one Jew
and that'll
be it
just one Jew
and we'll
be saved,

and having had one
just one Jew
appetite grew
and grew
for one
more Jew
just another
one more Jew
to save us all
just one Jew,
the skulls
grew and grew
of just one more Jew
heaps of skulls
no more Jews,
not ever
just one
more Jew

Donna Pucciani

After the Earthquake

Around the table, we drink coffee
in small cups, peel oranges
with little knives. Crumbs of cake
dot the blue cotton tablecloth
like chunks of houses all over Umbria
felled in the streets.

Just when the pieces of our lives
fall into place, another tremolo
sets us afire, breaks us into pieces
where our fears multiply.
The lights flicker. Television falters.
I look up at the wooden beams,
imagine them crushing us,
leaving the house roofless
where concrete used to be.

But for now, we are safe and whole.
The sheep still in the valley, the bees
swarming in the apiary on the hill
as though nothing has happened,
nothing at all.

THE DISCIPLINE OF GRATITUDE

I am told to be grateful
as I wake each morning
wrapped in the unfolding blanket of dawn,
shake off the moon, dying stars,
and taste the beige-gray breath
of incipient day.

Grateful to whom or what?
To the rain that coats the pavement
with its timid sheen, the birds' silence
in the settling damp, the bodies
of neighbors rising, reluctant,
in boxes of houses that line the street
with woe and weariness?

Let me drink strong coffee,
toast my bread with dailiness,
uncurl myself to a day lit only
by a hidden sun. I might have been
rich or famous, cured cancer,
saved the world. For now,
let me watch butter
melt as a golden flower.

ADVENT

Hands can catch
water from a stream

for drinking or the gathering
of stones, or the feel of something

cold, pure, elemental.
Grasping the dark is harder.

Winter's rough air
slips through outstretched fingers.

Unembraceable night
fills with wisps of wanting,

thoughts of old lovers, the dead
and dying, falling through space.

Our open palms hold only
lamentations. We await

the promise of fire, receive only
darkness,

and bow under it, bow to it,
the unseen star.

END TIMES

The doctors say
we are all terminal.
We swallow pills,
navigate blood-soaked terrain.

The Reaper pokes his head in
to ask directions. We lift
our lanterns, stare out startled
into the dark.

Our bodies will enter earth and fire,
the dust from which we came.
We fall into the mouths of old lovers,
ride the wings of dragonflies.

We seek one last embrace,
the taste of an apple,
the comfort of an old coat,
a page from an unfinished book.

We are the one-eyed cat
and the three-legged dog,
limping into a world that has
awaited us secretly and forever.

We lie down, close our eyes,
wait for the saffron sun.

DE-ICING THE PLANE

A small black truck huddles
behind one wing, buried in a shroud

of smoke. Exhaust fumes? fire?
No. A cloud of detergent

billows over the plane. When every suitcase
is stowed, every seat belt buckled,

and the runways plowed, the black truck
sidles up again, the airport's winter "familiar."

The silver bird, with floury faces ovalled
on its side, slithers into a blizzard, hugely blind.

No mincing steps, no Lot's wife here.
One hesitation could mean death

ablaze on a snowy superhighway. Everyone
prays, "Up, up," to the engine's crescendo,

like sparrows sudsed in a birdbath
just before flight.

Sarah Rossiter

BAPTISMAL PRAYER

This is the season when trees
Stand naked, stamped in sharp
Shadow on still-green grass.
This is the time between living
And dying.

Grant me an inquiring and
Discerning heart,

This is the human season now;
The air turns cold, and, daily,
Darker. Turkeys strut, circling,
Raw necks extended. Who
Knows what comes next.

The courage to will and
To persevere,

A threshold time between hope
And despair. A thousand joys,
A thousand sorrows. There is no
Escape from death. There is no
Escape from life.

The spirit to know and
To love you,

The last leaf lingers on the asters.
Suet hangs from the redbud tree.

This is the season when dusk comes
Early. Wind sings in the willows.
The night stars gather.

And the gift of joy and wonder
In all your works.

IN THE BEGINNING
Everything in the world begins with a yes.
—Clarice Lispecter

For Bishop Tom

In the beginning there is only Yes,
infinitesimal, infinite, invisible
seed sprouting in the swirling dark,
the slow integration, expanding,
extending, the sudden explosion
into light—baby, blossom, universe,
all beginnings are the same—and Yes
to a world begun before words where
nothing separates this from that, and
Yes to the senses alive before language,
bird song, leaf shadow, skin touching
skin, and Yes to Tom whose ravaged
brain erases speaking, reading, names,
but through hands cupped upon bent
heads, the unimpeded heart pours forth,
there's nothing to restrict the flow of
Yes in beginning and Yes in the end.

WINTER

This is the season:
Cradle of quiet,
Trees, waiting,
Naked on the hill,
Branches entwined
Like lovers holding
Hands.

Nothing is hidden.
A lone leaf quivers
On the apple tree.
Snow has yet to fall.
Waiting, the grass
Lies mute.

It could be death but
Isn't. Yet. Wings
Quicken serrated air
As nuthatch, junco,
Chickadee flit from
Tree to tree, oblivious
To the hawk circling
Overhead, waiting,
Like the grass, for what
Comes next.

And it will come,
To all of us—there's
No exception—

But if that frightens
You, hold it like
A stone beneath
The tongue until
It softens, and
You realize that
Nothing is ever lost
But is, instead,
Transformed as one
Door opens to another,
As even now light
Lifts the shadows,
And, out of sight,
Sap, wakeful, whispers
In the apple tree.

MOURNING

In early March
the doves mourn
as each new dawn
I sit, looking over
the barren field
where for ten days
nothing stirs until
six weeks from
the day she died,
an owl flies from
dark woods to perch
on a bare branch
above the Buddha
where, motionless,
his round unblinking
eyes stare into mine
though who knows
what he sees, or what,
if anything, it means,
but life is like that,
isn't it, the way it
sometimes when least
expected breaks wide
open, and what appeared
as lost is found.

THE BODY OF THE WORLD

When spring comes,
The Body wakes,
Flesh of our flesh
Without whom nothing
Would exist.

Mother to all,
Raccoon, fish, flower,
No need neglected,
Food, warmth, water.

The Body stirs,
Buds quicken, sprout,
Green softens hills,
Trees blossom, fruit.

The womb in which
We have our being,
The dearest freshness
Deep down things.

Each spring reborn,
The Body rises.
The source of life,
Praise Her. Praise Him.

Tania Runyan

NO ONE CAN BOAST

On the tollway just south of Kenosha
spring sets the boarded-up porn store ablaze,
topaz dousing the peeling paint,
the harp-notes of ice on the gutters.
On the embankment home geese gather
in the mud-slush. Tractors lift their beams
to the rising temple of a new overpass.

I outlasted winter, four months rumpled
under snow. On Christmas we woke
to a broken furnace, the baby's fingers
carrot-stick cold. One night I skidded
off the patio steps. Most mornings I stared
out the window, wondering how far
I'd driven my life in the ground,
asking the darkness how much longer.

I kill the radio. Just the hum of the motor,
the pitted road, my slow, steady breath
like the syllables *Yah, weh.* I didn't work
at this joy. It just appeared in the splash
and shine of I-94, as suddenly as these Frisbees
and sand buckets in the roadside yards
laid bare by the shrinking snow.

THE EMPTY TOMB
—*John 20*

That *woman* was the first word spoken
must have taken even the angels by surprise,

who were used to bringing their fiery glory
down to the clanging swords of battlefields,

to priests tugging at their beards
in lamentation, to voices thundering in temples

and muscles hefting stones from mountaintops,
not to a trembling woman whose hair clung

to her neck with tears, who for a moment
held the souls of the nations like a basket of figs.

MAN IS WITHOUT EXCUSE

Perhaps you could say that in Rome, Paul,
where the olive trees of the Seven Hills

strung their pearls of rain against the sky.
And yes, as I hike Glacier Park

with a well-stocked pack, I can welcome
God's ambassadors of fireweed and paintbrush,

the psalmic rhythm of lake hitting shore.
But as the refugee trudges

from Mogadishu to Dabaab, is she to catch
a glimpse of antelope bone in the thicket

and intuit the sufferings of the Son of Man?
She wears her own nails and crown.

An Eden of lizards surges at her heels,
but she wonders at nothing

but the sore-studded daughter she left to die
on the road, and now, the baby

strapped to her back: six pounds
at one year old. He no longer cries

but flutters small breaths on her neck
like the golden wings of moths

she counts with worshipful attention.

COUNT IT ALL AS LOSS

All of it: children whistling ryegrass,
my husband rubbing my back

in his sleep. Consider rubbish the sun
climbing the eye of Delicate Arch,

the scent of popped-open coffee.
Leave it behind, pleads the scourge-

scarred Paul. Lay it down and rise.
But even loss is hard to count as loss.

This morning frost has leathered
the nasturtium, but I cannot endure

ripping the haloes of leaves from their pot.
The astilbe, once a lavender mist

in my window, burns toward winter,
seed heads trembling like the hands

of an old charismatic. Maybe in heaven
I will remember the March I buried

those bare roots around the base of the oak
and brooded about some sin or another

holding me fast in the mud, spring
the only unseen I could bear to believe.

SONNET FOR MYSELF AT 17

To the one I love, who played violin
and twirled your hair with gracious angst:
You pried clean off your grip on sin
to sing with far and wide and deep. And lost.

You didn't realize black and white would blind
you. That Tchaikovsky's music pours from light
despite vodka and trysts with men to bind
him. *You're either for or against the word of Christ.*

But didn't you know Jesus rolled into view
every time you underlined sadnesses in books
you couldn't explain? His words, so hidden and new
bloomed from the gray, the silt-specked muck.

You drew your bow across a weary string.
The notes were always right but didn't ring.

THE SPIRIT SEARCHES EVERYTHING

Endless darknesses of deep space and sea
Verify something super holy's going on
Even when your lost-in-the-middle life
Needs a shot of sanctity.

Take your mind, for instance.
How long has it been since a new note or color
Ebbed at the edges of it, or you

Dredged up one of those groaning prayers only
Egrets and demons understand? The biggest
Part of the problem is just getting out of bed—
Taking your meds and hauling a comb through your
Hair. But even that can launch your legion into
Swine, or turn your cortisol into a fine merlot

Or bind up your broken heart in the whirling
Fringe of his hem. Watch. When there's nothing

Going for you, God will flip himself inside
Out, toss his guts on the floor, and only you will
Divine it. That's kind of the point.

Luci Shaw

CATCH OF THE DAY

It leaps, breaking the skin of the lake
of possibility, this thing that flashes steel—
this trout of a poem, wild with life, rainbow scales
and spiny fins. Now, for patience, the pull of the catch:

I cast, wait for the tug—the jerk of the hook in bony jaw—
feel the line go taut. The ballet begins, a wrestle
to land this flailing, feral thing—all thrash and edge—
and tame it into telling its own muscular story.

I heave it over the edge of its arrival, glorious,
fighting the whole way, slippery as language.
Its beauty twitches on the floor boards, its glisten
spilling over the bottom of my notebook page.

COMEBACK FOR SNOWY PLOVER
Associated Press headline, Oct. 13, 2014

O, lesser flake of feathers, O downy
shore-winged picker of cockles

and mites, twig-legged runner through ripples,
who was it called you out of extinction

to flit and flirt again with the waves?
Who missed you enough to amend

your habitation? Who restored you,
winging you back to the beaches of our lives?

What urgent impulse then spirited you,
safe in your dappled egg—to break shell,

chick stirring in shallow sand-scrape,
lifting to fly the salt wind, rising in drifts

over wild surf, your pinions
riding the breath of God?

CONTEMPLATIVE PRAYER WITH PEONY

So, I didn't latch onto a holy word
and go into space and, ethereal,
lose touch with my body. But God,
in those thirty slow minutes, you
unfolded in me the bud of a fresh
flower, with color and fragrance
that was more than my soul
was capable of, on its own.

> *. . . We all, with unveiled face,*
> *behold as in a mirror*
> *the glory of the Lord.*

And when the peony showed up,
I saw it as a kind of lens for vision.
This was glory in pink and cream, with
a smell of heaven. Petals like valves
opening into the colors of my heart.

I saw myself kneeling on a grass border,
my knees bruising the green, pressing
my face into the face of this silken,
just-opened bloom, and breathing it,
wanting to drown in it. Wanting
to grow in its reflected image.

WHERE COLOR IS SPARE

Where color is spare
we are given shape
and shade. Angles matter,
the up-thrust of a rock,
the way horizons
map the earth even in the dark.

Early, in the stillness before birds,
we feel our way, knowing
the slick of floor tiles in
the bathroom, the jut of corner,
the slant of closet door,
its handle like a friend's firm grip.

The reach for the railing
for confidence down the stairs.
The button to push to wake
the coffee maker.

The light switches that we
decide to not use. Yet.
Allowing the lovely mystery
of impression.

TESTIMONY

Though my hearing is never
acute enough to detect
the soft script of the fly's footfalls
as it dances on the window,
and cleans its wings with its
hind legs, the glass knows. The air
records it in a single instant,
irreversible.

Like my mother's voice when she
spoke harshly. The whisper of
small roughage, and only crumbs
left on the table between us.

MARY CONSIDERS HER SITUATION

What next, she wonders,
with the angel disappearing, and her room
suddenly gone dark.

The loneliness of her news
possesses her. She ponders
how to tell her mother.

Still, the secret at her heart burns like
a sun rising. How to hold it in—
that which cannot be contained.

She nestles into herself, half-convinced
it was some kind of good dream,
she its visionary.

But then, part dazzled, part prescient—
she hugs her body, a pod with a seed
that will split her.

J. Barrie Shepherd

THE STATION BAND
RAF Binbrook – 1953

We practiced at "The Decontam"—
clumsy name for an ugly place—bare concrete rooms
buried beneath a protective pyramid mound of soil, turf,
and God knows what, designated sanctuary nonetheless
for any unlucky enough, "in the event of nuclear attack,"
to survive the initial blast and burn to reach this subterranean
space of hollow refuge. The Station Decontamination Centre—
to rhyme the place in full, an—as yet—unfrequented location
(praises be!) where, Tuesday nights, an ill-assorted crew
of horns and woodwinds—sackbuts, cornets, clarinets,
even the occasional bassoon, would fumble-stumble along
through "Colonel Bogey," "The RAF March Past," old favorites
from Gilbert and Sullivan, "Chu Chin Chow," and Noel Coward,
rehearsing for the CO's garden party, full-dress dinner evenings
at the Mess. They echoed so, those naked rooms and corridors,
as if our music might drown out—yes, decontaminate—the fury
cradled tight beneath the wings of our sleek avenging bombers;
full squadrons perched above in laden readiness,
paying no heed to our hapless melodies and marches.

BOMB FRAGMENT
(on my study wall)

Sixty years ago and more
you fell black from the open belly
of a Heinkel or a Junkers over Yorkshire
in the siren-panicked night, slammed tight
into the crisp topped tar-macadam
of our new suburban Drive,
and burned your little liquid hell of hate—
incendiary white—across the melting gravel chips
where, just last week, I had skinned my knees
in falling from a bike.

Dad, the Air Raid Warden,
bore you home in an old moldy sack
to show his buried boys, deep in the backyard
air-raid shelter just what the war was all about,
while Dick—the younger one—woke up in fright
and vomited his supper in the damp and earthy dark.

Before he died Dad entrusted you to me,
"As the oldest. . . "—how he put it—
"the one who remembers." So you became an heirloom,
one of very few, along with the brass nameplate
from the door of my Scots baker granddad's house.
Until now, in a still darker, doom-divining season,
I test your heft against my praying palm,
and sense, beneath the skin, a conflagration
once evaded, that awaits its fated—
almost final—moment to consume.

FOREST SNOWFALL
Before Sunrise

It is as if the light that is to come
had taken on a flake-like form and substance
laid itself, in silhouette, along, against,
the windward part
of every naked trunk and branch.
The ground below lies cloaked,
each blade of grass or bracken
with its glistening garment,
so that, even at the darkest hour last night,
a luminescence shone as if reflected
from whatever burns within.

Might the bright, promised realm
lie here and now revealed,
its last impediment
my faltering fear to enter in?

TOCSIN

"a warning; an omen . . ."
—*American Heritage Dictionary*

Here on Maine's rocky coast we should not be too surprised
to hear the occasional shrill melody, a sand piper, perhaps,
or endangered piping plover, sounding the alarm
from Higgins Beach just down the shore.
But these recent evenings we are being serenaded—
late but lusty—by this year's crop of peeper frogs,
piping their insistent, somehow eerie clamor from the reeds
that cluster round our catchment pond, there by the dog run.
"Singing for their supper, like as not." I reassure myself,
as their steep voices punctuate my final dog walk of the day;
although—more likely—singing for something a tad closer
to this fast approaching bed-time, bedding-down-time—
what I mean—clambering-upon-time, time for frogs to do
their clinging, slippery, slimy thing that leads to further frogs;
a not inconsequential process for this lately threatened species.
"We piped to you . . . you did not dance," was what the holy man said
long ago, . . . "we wailed . . . you did not weep."
So are they also wailing over there tonight, and is anyone,
apart from my small dog, panicked by their urgent, haunting cries?

WORLDLY WISDOM?

I'm still looking, scanning,
skipping right to the end at times,
or settling for the gist on the first page,
reading—more selectively across the years—
but reading just the same, in the news
and novels, articles and extracts, poems even . . .
searching for the one, the word, the sentence
that can tell me what it's all about,
why I'm here, will not be here much longer,
where this morning's golden-leaving
autumn beauty comes from,
why, and what it's for,
who thought this whole thing called existence up
and maybe has a clue about its shape
and size and possible duration.
While all the time, beneath, behind,
beyond the endless pages,
the unrelenting streaming of the words,
it unquestionably happens,
keeps on happening,
without any hope or need for explanation,
moving on, while I stand wordless,
gasping in its tumbling wake.

EASTER ALONE

There is something to be said for solitary.
Those initial appearances, you may recall,
were not made before acclaiming throngs
with sounding brasses, immaculate ranks
of lilies, golden banners, alleluias
and the like, but to one or two, three
at the most, battered, broken souls
seeking solace for their grief and fear.

This morning's virus-isolated sunrise,
plague bare of all the customary celebration,
friendly handshakes, warm embraces—
He is risen. . . risen indeed!—finds me
at Atlantic's edge, sole company
the occasional chickadee, my foraging terrier,
light breeze and gentle waves against
the rocks my organ repertory,
awakening bird song through the trees
my antiphonal call and response.

No one was missing.
This vast community of life and light,
flowing liquid and unyielding rock,
one immense, eternal benediction,
holding me close—despite—
informing me—full and clear—
that all is given, all is now,
and everything is yet to be.

Anya Silver

AFTER THE BIOPSY

*"Each time that we have some pain to go through, we
can say to ourselves quite truly that it is the universe,
the order and beauty of the world, and the obedience of
creation to God that are entering our body. After that,
how can we fail to bless with tenderest gratitude the Love
that sends us this gift?"*
—Simone Weil

The pathology report an icon; the tissue
staining the slide, God's kaleidoscope.
And those cells, obeying their DNA,
cosmic dust as they whirl and split.
Why not praise cancer, relentless, blind,
that seeks and finds the lymph and blood?
Because I am unthankful, rude.
Because if I linger over this gift,
I will change, I will vanish from the earth.
In Russia, an icon of Mary has wept
for twenty years. Mary, do you see
my nuclei mutating, like words
in "whisper down the lane"? This same God
took your son away. Help me disobey.

COINCIDENCE

The same morning I press my shorn chest
flat against an x-ray machine, my sister
pushes from her body a baby girl.
Praise God, whose hand passes over itself
like river currents as it gives and takes,
pulls one film from the whirring machine
while pushing in a new, unprinted slide.
Praise God for this fearful doubling, over
which I will sometimes weep and curse.
Little breathing at the still whole breast
of my sister, little gold seed of death
awakening as the first sun touches its tendrils.

ON OUR ANNIVERSARY

The Quaker Meeting House in which we wed
was shabby—its carpet faded Wedgewood blue,
no festive flowers in a vase, or ribboned pews.
But I loved the butter-yellow stucco walls,
and the little graveyard at the back, ivy-grown,
where only the tops of squat square stones shown
grey above the vines. Beneath the eaves, we held
for view our newly golden fingers, the charms
through which we'd changed from two to one.

We knew a great thing had been done.
We were to be each other's rune and grail,
trunk and totem, handkerchief and spoon.
Forsaking sex with all others, refusing
escape alone from trouble, we promised to cling
to the human whom we'd named and kissed.
And what a wonder that we did, and have, that years
have proved us braver than we knew, and merry,
too, love still searching out each other's hands,
as when, beneath the poplars' summer green,
we walked from vows to wedding cake and dancing,
and cars drove in the street below the underpass,
distracted, to their many destinations.

HOLY, HOLY, HOLY

How to love the Trinity, its vagueness,
non-sense, God talking to God on the cross?
Theological geometry, stumper of metaphor,
God humbled to a peanut butter and jelly sandwich.
Only when I heard that voice singing *Our songs*
shall rise to thee did I feel a welling of love
that, at best, visits me occasionally in prayer,
indwelling and expanding within me.
Yes, God, *the darkness hideth thee.*
Too often as I sit in the pews, nothing
happens. Or worse, Nothing happens,
doubt a scrim over every word I pray,
a tepid mutter of *Father, Son, and Holy Spirit.*
But that hymn's falsetto, surrender, the not-
knowingness of it—Lord, though I can not see,
I did hear a shimmer, some wick in me caught
fire, and fear, that liar, left me, momentarily,
free in the Holy, music, the blessed Trinity.

For S. S.

PSALM 137 FOR NOAH

Come darling, sit by my side and weep.
I have no lyre, no melodious voice or chant.
I meditate on the Zion I could never grant you.
My son, my roe deer, my rock-rent stream.
My honeysuckle, my salt, my golden spear.
Forgive me your birth in this strange land.
I wanted your infant kisses, your fists clasped
round my neck. I craved you, though you were born
in the wake of my illness, my dim prognosis.
I was selfish: I willed you this woe, this world.
You inherited exile for my sake.

Bill Stadick

RUBENS WOULD NEED A LIGHT SOURCE

They knew.
The famous always know they are watched.
They understood their positions
around the manger mattered, that even
in an unlit cranny of creation, someone
somewhere would record with paint or pen
every head tilt and cow grunt.

Mary, for example, knew. She wrinkled
her pink gown just so, joyed up her eyes just so
and squared her biceps around him just so
for the benefit of Rubens. Then she scurried
over straw for Botticelli's sake and lined up
steer, then steed, then herself, remembering
to clasp her hands just in time above the Lord-Is-Come.

Joseph also knew. He shifted with mock
stage-fright from foot to foot,
glancing at the Messiah as though
a plastic-faced doll
because someday this would serve as model
everywhere for Sunday school pageants.

Even the holy infant knew,
as he squinched his eyes tighter
and tighter, gushing a nimbus
with museum-worthy brilliance
from his pores (Rubens would need
a light source and it might as well be him).

Taking advantage of his useless,
newborn neck muscles, the little
Lord Jesus next experimented
with a series of head flops
to be perfected at some later date
on a hill far away.

Advent 1995

THE DOS AND DON'TS OF BURYING ME
Let goods and kindred go.

Don't, my townspeople,   hype the hyphen,
those fill-in-the-blah-blah-blank   years
between some b and its   subsequent d.
No prattling on   of how I   scribble-shilled for salaries,
of how I shuttled my several   offspring thither

after quick stops at some   hither or other,
of how I ballpointed   almost-subversive verse
around potluck   save-the-dates
in Baptist bulletins.   None of that
celebration of life la-tee-da I'm dead now.

Neither gush how much I   loved wife,
daughter, son, daughter, son,   Son
of God and the 2016 Chicago   Cubs with
intermittently appropriate   intensities.
No need to whitewash   *this* tomb.

But do, my townspeople,   articulate
the doctrine of alien   righteousness
over my corpus   so lucidly
Lucifer can't   conceal
a lingering scowl   and Luther

gets one last jowl-   jiggling laugh
as he Oktoberfest-sings, *The just*
shall LIVE,   shall LIVE,   shall LIVE   by faith.
Likewise, all of you sing   *My hope is built*
on nothing less than   Jesus' blood

and righteousness   and mean it
as much as I did   at 16,
by which happy   birthday
I'd already made a hash   of mine own.
Next, do stand together   and sing

and in and out of   tune
In Christ Alone.   Last
read Hebrews   6:13-20
loud as a   street preacher
and know I   made eternal book

on the   existence / promise / oath
of this God and it's my pre-
destined *we are beggars   'tis true*
moment to see how   this celebration
of afterlife   hallelujahs   out.

THE SIN-BOLDLY-BULWARK-NEVER-FAILING BLUES

I just   opened the can of worms that will eat my flesh

I just   shrugged *it's all good* and my nose started Pinnochioing

I just   passed my annual physical and failed my annual spiritual

I just   peeked into my closet and one of its skeletons whispered
         It's me, Uriah

I just   vomited after winning a humble pie eating contest

I just   tried talking my way out of eternal damnation as I would a
         parking ticket

I just   called to say I'm sorry (I got caught)

I just   justified shouting *raca* at my neighbor because his fallen
         leaves transgressed boundaries

I just   can't stop myself from saying *I just*

I just   confronted all my demons and they doggedly refused to
         settle out of court

I just   plugged in another household god that's blaring *mea culpa
         non. mea maxima culpa non*

I just   remembered 1521

I just   reread Habakkuk 2:4

I just   ordered me a heaping helping of alien righteousness

I just   keep repeating *hier stehe, ich kann nicht anders* and *yum*

THE HEAD USHER STARTS SEEING THINGS

Not the powder-blue tithe
envelopes nor the registration
cards nor even the mussed

currency in these plates but
the dishes themselves
thrill me as my lackeys

stack them sternum-high
in my two upturned palms.
and I can't stop my imagination

from overlaying across
the top of them a pie chart
with the ten color-coded slices

of our annual budget. But then
a single settles and George's
crinkled eyes wink, I swear,

at me and morph into
two, I swear, of that
pesky widow's mites.

A DEAD MAN'S BIBLE

I lazy-paged through it when he was done
With it for all eternity and read
His penciled margin notes. Each seventh one
Had misspelled words (e.g., a *lead* for *led*).
These savvy days, of course, one should do better
(Although I'm confident no beryl jewels
In his gold crown were compromised). Paul's letter
Concluded (paraphrasing here) we're fools
In this world's eyes, dull dregs who write in square,
Prim capitals, just Eds who nervous-teach
Our fifth-grade Sunday schools, forgetting where
We placed next thoughts. So odd today to reach
Inside my couplet bag—they're all but gone—
While he's off somewhere penning a new song.

(In memoriam EWS, 1932–2001)

Bonnie Thurston

WAS BLIND, BUT NOW I SEE

You have your sight, and yet you cannot see
—Teiresias, *Oedipus Rex*

Driving into the city to teach
in gray-green late summer,
I see one flaming red maple
and think of Oedipus
standing dangerously above the *hoi polloi.*

But it is Moses' tree,
a call story on a highway hillside.
I want to stop traffic,
shout, "take off your shoes, people!"

For the world is on fire
with a beauty so fragile that,
like the thread of ash
after the stick of incense burns,
one breath can topple it.

THE SOUND OF LIGHT

Hindus call it *shabd,*
and Sufis know it, too,
the Divine Light
(Hopkins' dazzling darkness?)
that falls from heaven
on our midnight world,
or glows from within,
suffusing all creation,
making celestial music
only the wise and holy hear.

Behind the blue black mountains
dawn is unfurling
a bolt of rose velvet.
A line of birds blows
across the horizon
in a winter wind
that smells of snow.
Is it birds I hear
or the faintest *pianissimo*
of coming Light?

PASSING

I do not expect to breach heaven
(if there is some heaven
beyond our good, green earth)
via pearly gates, golden streets
with searchlights searing the sky
and something noisy from Handel
blaring from the speakers.

If at all, the passage will be
secretive and silent,
a chink through which I slip,
perhaps between the rose bud
and its fragrant flowering,
the moment when baton is lifted
before overture's first note sounds.

Rarely in gaudy glory of liturgy
as Host is elevated, eaten,
often in spring's gentle uncurling,
autumn's downward spiral,
I see a shadowy hand beckon,
or hear a quiet voice calling,
"This way. Slip through here."

EVE OF ADVENT

The few remaining leaves
stagger drunkenly, randomly
across the darkening sky.
The wind blows them
where it will, begins to moan
the loss of autumnal color,
mourn the coming darkness.
Christ comes in darkness,
ambiguous gift to a virgin mother.
Not for the likes of them
guiding stars, comfortable welcome,
only alien status in unknown Egypt
the result of an old man's dream
and then a promised piercing.
And yet we hymn them,
these three mismatched refugees,
long for their story's meaning,
for truth not propositional,
not even likely or reasonable,
ungraspable as leaves in the wind:
this radiance in an unlit cave.

WRONG WAY ROUND

In a theological tome I read
"opening the world to God"
which echoes in my ear
a quarter tone off pitch,
just enough to make choirs
of angels and archangels wince.

Surely that is backwards.
The whole amazing universe,
every minute or enormous thing,
is a door opening into God,
a summons to eternity
in a dust-to-dust creation,
an invitation to adoration,
the substance of forever.

Shari Wagner

OLIN LAKE

Behind us, the channel half-clogged
by bullhead lilies slips back
into the smoke of yellow tamaracks
clouding the shore. We glide
on the silk of a dream so deep, herring
break the surface from eighty feet below.

I am this hand skimming the water.
I am these eyes dazzled by light.

I am you whom I loved
before the continents were parted.

I am in the creak of wood,
old harmony of oars.

THE FARM WIFE FINDS HER NECKLACE IN THE JUNK DRAWER

That's what's left of it—
    six safety pins
from a chain I once wore
    beneath my dress to Saylor's
School and Forks Mennonite
    Church. Who'd suspect
vanity in a girl so shy
    she seldom spoke? I liked
how each pin clicked shut
    to link to the next
and how they encircled me
    like a charm of daisies
I counted round and
    round. Some would have said
that was a sin. The same
    folks who'd pocket a shiny
buckeye against the ache
    of rheumatism.
I took my necklace off
    when I joined my life
with Pete's. I needed pins
    for diapers, school notes,
lost buttons, loose straps—
    catastrophes
only the quick clasp
    of hidden silver fixed.

THE FARM WIFE EATS OUT AT MARNER'S SIX MILE CAFÉ

Widowed farmers cram the table
near the peanut butter pies,

but I prefer the back booth
beneath a pike framed with flowers.

Under a coffee cup's "Start your day
with Jesus," I find Topeka Seed & Stove.

Once, when it was crowded,
we ate in the kitchen where an Amish cook

beat the batter while flipping eggs
and watching toast. Annie doesn't bring

us menus. She knows the grandkids and I
will order pancakes with cinnamon butter

faces. When my sisters visit, they say,
"Let's go someplace with atmosphere."

They mean a chain near the interstate
where they decorate with sport stars

and license plates, where the booths
are so tall, you can't see your neighbors.

THE FARM WIFE LOOKS UP AT THE COSMOS

When it's too nice to nap indoors, I take
an old knotted comforter to the back edge
of the garden, near tomato leaves I crush
for a last whiff of summer. Crickets chorus
round me and the combine's racket turns
to a purr the barn cats pick up, settling
near my head. It's then I look up at the cosmos,
struck by their petals, mandarin orange
against blue sky. The underside shines
radiant as monarch wings or the stained glass
of sun through tissue paper. Resting
by County Road N 400 W, I forget
laundry on the line, supper to fix.
For hours I've been napping. Now I am awake.

THE FARM WIFE SHARES HER VIEW ON WINDOWS IN THE NEW SANCTUARY

Some members are voting for clear glass
while others believe frosted would be nicer.

I prefer a view of Ed Troyer's cows
and a way to survey the sky. It gives me pause

to think of everyone in the same room
with no way to look out and no sunlight

crossing the pews. Call the outside a distraction,
but I'd rather pray with the Amish in a barn,

the big door flung open and swallows with forked
tails, darting in and out. I'm saying this softly

because even Mennonites who favor clear glass
might see some taint of worldliness, unsettling

as the stained glass in the old sanctuary
when it was Methodist. Sam Troyer, Ed's father,

loaded those windows on a wagon headed
for the dump, but he took a wrong turn. Now

no one in LaGrange County has a prettier
barn than Ed's. You should see the milking parlor,

how lilies of the field hold the light.

THE FARM WIFE COLLECTS FREQUENT FLYER MILES

I find my seat on a gray plank
        and grasp stout rope tied
to a sycamore branch. Leaning back,
           I pump till I'm lifting off.

over barbed wire, dusty beans,
        six-foot corn, my legs stretched
to spin the rusty rooster's arrow.
           I reach for what I see

and what I don't. The wind in my face
        whispers, *Esther, Esther,*
or is it you, my heart, pumping
           as I pump that speaks? "I'm here,"

I say, like faithful Samuel
        answered in the darkness.
Leaning into the arms of this world
           that push me forward, I forget

stiff arthritis and varicose veins.
        I let go of the back and forth
of brooms and mops, sweepers and irons
           and rock with the bliss

a rocking chair rocks or a pendulum
        swinging from the sun.

Jeanne Murray Walker

HELPING THE MORNING

After the grave, after the ride home, after
    a winter of drought, the chain
        and padlock on my heart,

morning shows up at my bedside,
    almost too late, like a big sister
        holding a glass of water

and I drink, glancing through the window
    at the tiny red barn flung
        into the lap of the brown valley below.

I am amazed at the silent, terrible wonder
    of my health. I am giddy at the lack of war.
    I want to help the morning.

I pray the bedpost, the windowpanes.
    I put our children on two doorknobs,
        Our sick friends in mirrors.

Like the aperture of a camera, the morning opens
    and keeps opening until the room is filled
        with rosy light and I could believe

anything: that grass might turn green again,
    that a cloud the size of my hand
        might swell, drift in, bringing rain.

VAN GOGH

All right, I love him for the way
            he painted *Vermilion! Orange!* Jagged as
      shouts, and when no one bought them,
          no one even heard him,
he shouted louder,
          Sunflowers! Self Portrait!
And years later, not one sold,
        he cut off his own ear.

Then he had to bring it back on canvas
          hundreds of times,
     in the brass swelling
       of the bell
that called him to dinner,
      in the complicated iris
          at the end of the asylum path.
            Think how stooping
at a fork in the road
         he might have seen a stone-shaped ear,
     how the human heart,
         once it knows what it needs,
will find it everywhere, how
      in the curve of his delicately padded cell
          one starry night, he must have murmured
            everything he had ever wanted to say
straight into the ear of God.

LITTLE BLESSING FOR A SUICIDAL CHILD

I am driving in late day sunlight
when a girl in a silver car aims
for me and quick as an email
from hades, sails to my address.
Her stare obliterates me, empties
my driver's seat. So fervently
does she want me out of her way,
she seems happy to be canceled too,
and I quickly hope that death
will oblige the lust she feels for it.
An opulence of loathing
fills me. Full throttle hatred,

until I see her mouth, her suffering
frown, how exposed she is, wearing
only the flimsy dress of that car,
her brief face etched and dying on
the air. And as I swerve from her path,
a voice speaks through me: *May
her parents see her face alive
again.* It amazes me, my own
voice and changes me.

RITUAL

If God is the newest thing, the youngest
thing, as Meister Eckhart said, then look,
He's here, as my son hands baby Maggie
to the priest, who crosses her with water
like an X in tick tack toe. She enters the 0
of life through the mud-room of birth

fontanelle with God's good creature, water.
See, while she sleeps on, how fragile she is,
open to being pierced or blessed,
while outside the bright air trembles and a bell
starts clanging the whole sky to pieces.

CLUTTER

I am finally down
to what I need: one
table to double
for eating/writing,
one pen, and enough
alphabet to spell
Your name when
You choose to
disclose it.

Paul Willis

ALL SAINTS

November dawns the cool side of sunny,
and I walk to class thinking what I might suggest
to the eight young writers around the long, dark table.
I could point out once again that the walls in our room
are made of windows, that mountains are trying to get in.

Or I might say, "The soccer coach greeted me
in the parking lot in high spirits. His team is going
to the playoffs; his father, however, is dying of cancer."
Or I might say, "The Filipino maintenance man
asked me this morning what I am teaching.

'Shakespeare,' I told him. 'Is Shakespeare in the arts?'
he asked. 'Does he write opera? Is he an American?'"
Or perhaps I could share my sorrow about the Korean
pitcher who lost a World Series game in Yankee Stadium
last night. It was midnight, Halloween, there in

Yankee Stadium, but for all of his countrymen
in Korea, it was two o'clock in the afternoon.
In Korea, it had been November for a long time
when the ball sailed into the stands and the pitcher
placed his black glove like a dark flower upon his face.

Extra Innings

From a shaky scaffold rising out of the poison oak,
a pair of men are tearing off
the back of our redwood baseball stands.

Who would have guessed it?
Between the boards, row on row of honeycombs,
packed in like a visiting team in brown and saffron uniforms.

All these years a sweetness
building at our backs, a hidden infield
of play, the score kept in numberless columns

by so many runs home. Here was a game
never called on account of darkness,
only halted by too much light.

Cousin Quartet

Years ago, my mother sang in a quartet
with her sister Lorraine and their two cousins.
The Cousin Quartet, it was called.
I just asked her about it tonight, as she lay dying.

"The funny thing was," she said,
"we always stood with our backs to a window.
And someone was always pouring sand."

I asked my aunt about these things;
she shook her head. And so we gather
evidence for the fading music

of the mind, the light behind us.
And someone is always pouring sand.

INTERCESSION

When I wake in the night and think
of what I might have said in class that day,
I wonder why my life consists

of inarticulate occasions.
No timely word, only belated ones.
Every hour a first draft, and then another.

It makes me want to announce, *Listen!*
Listen to what I do not say. Listen
to what it is you cannot say yourselves.

There are sighs and groans,
just sighs and groans.
Interpret them, dear ones, as you may.

DROUGHT

The laurel sweeps its lower limbs
all the way down the rock
and into the creek that wasn't there
till last week's rainstorm.

If leaves could speak—
and they do, in their everlasting fragrance—
they would welcome the sound of water
traveling over sandstone.

The leaves would say,
We missed you—for almost a year,
you were gone. Please stay this time.
And the water would say, *Maybe. See ya.*

WE'RE BACK

After the fire, houses in the chaparral
start up again like new shoots of poison oak.
The resilience of nature? The power
of habit? The shallows of the human mind?

We keep building on the flood plain,
kicking steps up the avalanche chute,
camping out on the crumbling
lip of the volcano.

Those hollow figures at Pompeii,
crouched in the admission of error,
became the casts for Rodin's *Thinker*.
Think about it.

In Korea, there are a hundred different men
who claim to be returned messiahs
(not counting their messiah wives)—
and thousands who erect their faith upon this sand.

And here in the U. S. of A., cutting sagebrush
in my yard, the dry winds parting my lips,
I feel right at home with the rest,
making do, claiming ground.

Christian Wiman

WHATEVER THE BIRDS WERE

Like a spirited theological colloquy between two people
whose faith has failed,

two trees, alders, whipped drastic in the gust
that subsided so suddenly it seemed each had inhaled, and stilled.

Whatever the birds were that flitted back and forth between them then,
they made a silver seeming noise.

A BREAK IN THE STORM

My sorrow's flower was so small a joy
It took a winter seeing to see it as such.
Numb, unsteady, stunned at all the evidence
Of winter's blind imperative to destroy,
I looked up, and saw the bare abundance
Of a tree whose every limb was lined with snow.
What I was seeing then I did not quite know
But knew that one mite more would have been too much.

GONE FOR THE DAY, SHE IS THE DAY

Dawn is a dog's yawn, space
in bed where a body should be,
a nectared yard, night surviving
in wires through which what voices,
what needs already move—and the mind
nibbling, nibbling at Nothingness
like a mouse at cheese:

Spring!

*

Sometimes one has the sense
that to say the name
God is a great betrayal,
but whether one is betraying
God, language, or one's self
is harder to say.

*

Gone for the day, she is the day
opening in and around me
like flowers she planted in our yard.
Christ. Not flowers.
Gone for the day, she is the day
razoring in with the Serbian roofers,
and ten o'clock tapped exactly
by the one bad wheel of the tortilla cart,
and the newborn's noonday anguish

eased. And the tide the mind
makes of traffic and the bite
of reality that brings it back.
And the late afternoon afterlight
in which a much-loved dog lies
like a piece of precocious darkness
lifting his ears at threats, treats, comings, goings . . .

*

To love is to feel your death
given to you like a sentence,
to meet the judge's eyes
as if there were a judge,
as if he had eyes,
and love.

FOR D.

Groans going all the way up a young tree
Half-cracked and caught in the crook of another

Cease. All around the hill-ringed, heavened pond
Leaves shush themselves like an audience.

An atomic pause, as of some huge attention
Bearing down. May I hold your hand?

A clutch of mayflies banqueting on oblivion
Writhes above the water like visible light.

SMALL PRAYER IN A HARD WIND

As through a long-abandoned half-standing house
Only someone lost could find,

Which, with its paneless windows and sagging crossbeams,
Its hundred crevices in which a hundred creatures hoard and nest,

Seems both ghost of the life that happened there
And living spirit of this wasted place,

Wind seeks and sings every wound in the wood
That is open enough to receive it,

Shatter me God into my thousand sounds . . .

FROM ONE TIME

1. Canyon de Chelly, Arizona

Then I looked down into the lovely cut
of a missing river, something under dusk's
upflooding shadows claiming for itself a clarity
of which my eyes were not yet capable:
fissures could be footpaths, ancient homes
random erosions; pictographs depicting fealties
of who knows what hearts, to who knows what gods.
To believe is to believe you have been torn
from the abyss, yet stand waveringly on its rim.
I come back to the world. I come back
to the world and would speak of it plainly,
with only so much artifice as words
themselves require, only so much distance
as my own eyes impose. I believe
in the slickrock whorls of the real
canyon, the yucca's stricken clench,
and, on the other side, the dozen buzzards swirled
and buoyed above some terrible intangible fire
that must scald the very heart
of matter to cast up such miraculous ash.

2. 2047 Grace Street

But the world is more often refuge
than evidence, comfort and covert
for the flinching will, rather than the sharp
particulate instants through which God's being burns
into ours. I say God and mean more

than the bright abyss that opens in that word.
I say world and mean less
than the abstract oblivion of cells
out of which every intact thing emerges,
into which every intact thing finally goes.
I do not know how to come closer to God
but by standing where a world is ending
for one man. It is still dark,
and for an hour I have listened
to the breathing of the woman I love beyond
my ability to love. Praise to the pain
scalding us toward each other, the grief
beyond which, please God, she will live
and thrive. And praise to the light that is not
yet, the dawn in which one bird believes,
crying not as if there had been no night
but as if there were no night in which it had not been.

Carl Winderl

KNEELING AT THE MANGER

staffs at their sides, hushed

mouths agape, reeking not
of frankincense and myrrh, but

of linseed oil, sulfur, pitch, and
tar, these rough men
stare, stunned
by My Son's birth, shocked in

amazed gazing, at Him.

Their faces though I recognize, they're
the providers

of the Paschal lambs, at Passover

for the Temple, they breed and they
take from the ewes their firstborns to
bleed and suffer, sacrificed

to atone for Israel's sin, but

when their shepherd eyes meet mine
I see on their adoring faces a

glimpse of mute surprise, some

wonder; in an eyebrow's rise dis-
belief, while something

in their furtive sidelong glances
causes me to further ponder
more, for

they have been trained
to know a sacrificial lamb when

they see One

CONSTANTLY RISKING

absurdity and
death and
insanity, and

personal immortality

My Son so
performed His

miraculous acts

with no
safety net, neither
any thing up His
sleeve, nor even a
fire curtain

any where in sight

preferring to walk
a tight taut rope,

a Crimson Clown
an acrobat, not
an acrophobe
He trod

the thin wire of
Faith, like

walking on water

OH, HOW THE NEG—

ative reciprocals
abound and re-
dound in
of by through
around under and
out of

My Son's Life,

like the sad
sad story of
His Best olde
ex-friend judas

who went
into the
potter's field, fit
for a
plotter's grave

while on the re-
bound My Son
went into
a Potter's Grave
fit for

the Potter Himself

AS ONCE WAS SO

for danté
and virgil whence

they trespassed so

in the *Inferno*

'twas that was as
it was
for My Son, too

in his harrowing
of it . . .

on that Holy Saturday
when at
mid-*tierce*,
about 7:30

in the mourning,

mine, I
pondered, too

why, oh why
My God
hast thou forsaken

me, too?

but in no time I
would know not
to be
miss-taken,

for My Son
had only
descended therein
long enough

to forgive those
who trespassed

against Him

WHEN MY SON ROLLED

away the stone

sealed with
wax and guarded
by a pair
of rome's finest,

rolled it away far

far far away
from His
tomb's mouth

it rolled and
rolled and rolled
away over and
over until it

covered over for
-ever and ever

the Hole in
My Heart left by

simeon's sword

ABOUT THE POETS

Kim Bridgford (1959–2020) was an award-winning poet, professor, arts administrator, editor, fiction writer, and literary critic. She taught at Fairfield University in Fairfield, Connecticut, and at West Chester University in West Chester, Pennsylvania, where she served as director of the West Chester University Poetry Center. She was the founder and director of Poetry by the Sea: A Global Conference, the editor of *Mezzo Cammin* and founder of *The Mezzo Cammin Women Poets Timeline Project*. Bridgford was the author of many books of poetry, including *Bully Pulpit*, a book of poems on bullying; *Epiphanies, Doll,* and *A Crown for Ted and Sylvia*.

Peter Cooley is a native of the Midwest, and a graduate of Shimer College, the University of Chicago and the Writers' Workshop at University of Iowa, where he received his PhD. He has lived over half his life in New Orleans; he was Professor of English and Director of Creative Writing at Tulane University from 1975–2018. He has published eleven books of poetry, nine of them with Carnegie Mellon. His work has appeared in *The New Yorker, The Atlantic, The Nation, The New Republic* and in over one hundred anthologies. His eleventh book of poetry, *The One Certain Thing*, appeared in 2021. Cooley is the recipient of an ATLAS grant from the state of Louisiana and of the Marble Faun Poetry Award from the Faulkner Society in New Orleans. He is the Poetry Editor of *Christianity and Literature*, Professor Emeritus at Tulane University and former Louisiana Poet Laureate.

Barbara Crooker's work has appeared in a variety of journals, including *The Christian Century, Christianity & Literature, The Christian Science Monitor, America, Sojourners, Saint Katherine Review, Windhover, Perspectives, The Cresset, Tiferet, Spiritus, Assisi, Dappled Things, Ruminate, Rock & Sling, Radix,* and *Relief.* It's been anthologized in places like *The Bedford Introduction to Literature* (Bedford/St. Martin's), *Imago Dei: Poems from Christianity and Literature* (Abilene Christian University Press), *Looking for God in All the Right Places* (Loyola Press), and *Summer: A Spiritual Biography of the Season* and *Spring: A Spiritual Biography of the*

Season (SkyLights Paths Publishers). She is the author of nine books of poetry; *Some Glad Morning*, Pitt Poetry Series (University of Pittsburgh Poetry Press), is the latest.

Brian Doyle was a dad a dad a dad a husband, an editor, a sonbrotherfriend citizen and the author of twenty-nine books of essays, fiction, proems and explorations of hearts and vineyards. His last novel was *The Adventures of John Carson in Several Corners of the World* and in 2019, a collection of his breathtaking essays, *One Long River of Song* was published by Little Brown. His essays were reprinted far and wide, and of his many awards, a 2008 Award in Literature from the American Academy of Arts and Letters . . . was a total puzzle to him, although he got a free steak dinner out if it, in a lovely jazz club in Harlem, with a lovely and engaging dinner companion, what could be a better date than that, you know what I mean? Also he made the all-star team in a tough basketball league in Boston, but that was many years ago when the world was young and Dewey and there were no smart phones, yet.

Jill Alexander Essbaum is the award-winning author of several collections of poetry including *Heaven, Harlot, Necropolis*, and the single-poem chapbook *The Devastation*. Her first novel, *Hausfrau*, debuted on the New York Times Bestseller List and has been translated into 26 languages. Her work has appeared in dozens of journals including *Poetry, The Christian Century, Image*, and *The Rumpus*, as well as multiple Best American Poetry anthologies. A two-time NEA fellow, Jill is a core faculty member in The Low Residency MFA Program at University of California-Palm Desert. She lives in Austin, Texas.

Brett Foster (1973–2015) was Professor of English at Wheaton College and a past Wallace Stegner and Elizabethan Club fellow. His poetry and criticism has appeared in *Raritan*, the *Kenyon Review, Best New Poets 2007*, and *Books & Culture*, among other publications. His collection *Fall Run Road* was awarded Finishing Line Press's Open Chapbook Prize in 2011. His books *The Garbage Eater* (2011) and the posthumous *Extravagant Rescues* (2019) were both published by Northwestern University Press.

Nola Garrett is Faculty Emerita of Edinboro University of Pennsylvania. She lives in downtown Pittsburgh. She has received a Residency at Yaddo and Scholarships from White River Writers' Workshop, Bread Loaf Writers' Conference, West Chester Poetry Conference, and is listed on the *Mezzo Cammin Women Poets Timeline* and posted on *The Georgia Review's* "Vault." Her monthly blog/essays are available online at Autumn House Press coalhillreview.com. Her books include a collection of her sestinas, *The Dynamite Maker's Mistress*; *The Pastor's Wife Considers Pinball*; and *Ledge*.

Gracia Grindal is a retired professor of rhetoric at Luther Seminary in St. Paul, Minnesota. Her hymns and hymn translations are published in many hymnals including *Lutheran Book of Worship*. Her most recent book of poetry is titled *Jesus the Harmony, Gospel Sonnets for 366 Days*.

Malcolm Guite is an Anglican priest, poet, singer, song-writer and a Life Fellow of Girton College Cambridge. The author of seven books of poetry and seven books of theology and Christian faith, he also performs with the Cambridge-based rhythm and blues and rock band "Mystery Train."

Jeff Gundy is Distinguished Poet in Residence at Bluffton University. His thirteen books include *Wind Farm: Landscape with Stories and Towers,* an exploration of the Illinois landscape, history, and memoir in lyric essays and photographs, just out from Dos Madres Press. Other recent books include *Without a Plea* and *Abandoned Homeland* (both poems, from Bottom Dog Press) and *Songs from an Empty Cage: Poetry, Mystery, Anabaptism, and Peace* (criticism). His poems and essays appear in *Georgia Review, The Sun, Kenyon Review, Forklift, Ohio, Christian Century, Image, Cincinnati Review, Terrain,* and other journals. He held a Fulbright lectureship at the University of Salzburg in 2008 and was named Ohio Poet of the Year in 2015 for *Somewhere Near Defiance*.

Charles Hughes's two poetry collections are *The Evening Sky* and *Cave Art*, both from Wiseblood Books. His poems have appeared in *The Christian Century* and in other publications, including *Alabama Literary*

Review, America, the *Iron Horse Literary Review, Literary Matters,* and *Saint Katherine Review.* He worked as a lawyer for over thirty years before his retirement and lives in the Chicago area with his wife, Bunny Hughes, a Presbyterian pastor.

Jean Janzen, born in Canada and raised in the Midwest, has lived in Fresno, California, for sixty years, raised four children with her pediatrician husband, and began poetry writing with Philip Levine and Peter Everwine at Fresno State University in midlife. A recipient of an NEA grant, she has published seven poetry collections and two books of essays and has taught poetry writing at Fresno Pacific University and Eastern Mennonite University.

Philip C. Kolin, Distinguished Professor of English (Emeritus) and Editor Emeritus of the *Southern Quarterly* at the University of Southern Mississippi, has published more than 40 books, including ten collections of poems. Among the most recent are *Emmett Till in Different States: Poems* (Third World Press, 2015), *Reaching Forever: Poems* (Poiema Series, Cascade Books, 2019), and *Delta Tears: Poems* (Main Street Rag, 2021). His business and technical writing textbook *Successful Writing at Work* is now in its twelfth edition with Cengage Learning. His most recent book of poems is *Americorona* (Wipf & Stock, 2021).

Sydney Lea, a former Pulitzer finalist and winner of the Poets' Prize, served as founding editor of *New England Review* and was Vermont's Poet Laureate from 2011 to 2015. He is the author of 23 books, the latest of which is *Seen from All Sides: Lyric and Everyday Life,* essays. Fourteen of these volumes are poetry collections, the most recent of which is *Here* (Four Way Books, 2019). In 2021, he was presented with his home state of Vermont's most prestigious artist's distinction: the Governor's Award for Excellence in the Arts.

Karen An-Hwei Lee is the author of *Duress* (Cascade, 2022), *Rose is a Verb: Neo-Georgics* (Slant, 2021), *Phyla of Joy* (Tupelo, 2012), *Ardor* (Tupelo, 2008) and *In Medias Res* (Sarabande, 2004), winner of the Norma

Farber First Book Award. Currently, she serves as Provost and Professor of English at Wheaton College (Illinois).

Marjorie Maddox, winner of *America Magazine's* 2019 Foley Poetry Prize, Sage Graduate Fellow of Cornell (MFA), and Professor of English at Lock Haven University, has published 14 collections of poetry— including *Transplant, Transport, Transubstantiation* (Yellowglen Prize); *True, False, None of the Above* (Poiema Poetry Series, Illumination Book Award Medalist); *Begin with a Question* (Paraclete Press, International Book Award); and the ekphrastic collections *Heart Speaks, Is Spoken For*— with photographer Karen Elias—and *In the Museum of My Daughter's Mind*—based on 18 paintings by her daughter Anna Lee Hafer and other artists (Shanti Arts, 2022, 2023). In addition, she has published *What She Was Saying* (Fomite, stories); four children's and YA books—including *Inside Out: Poems on Writing and Reading Poems with Insider Exercises* (Kelsey Books, Finalist International Book Awards)—*Common Wealth: Contemporary Poets on Pennsylvania* (co-editor); and *Presence: A Journal of Catholic Poetry* (assistant editor).

Warren Lane Molton is an ordained minister who served churches in Washington, DC, and Connecticut, and as a chaplain in Korea. He was campus minister at the University of Connecticut, and then a seminary Professor of Pastoral Theology for six years before becoming a psychotherapist and founder of The Counseling Center for Human Development in Kansas City. He is the author of two books on marriage: *Friends, Partner and Lovers,* and *Spheres of Intimacy.* He also has published three collections of poetry: *Bruised Reeds, If God Is,* and *New Poems 2004-2012.* His poems have appeared in numerous magazines and journals, including *Theology Today,* and the Yale Divinity School's *Reflections,* and frequently in the *Christian Century* since 1956. For many years, he was poetry editor of *Pilgrimage, the Journal for Existential Psychology.* Warren and Mary Dian, his wife of seventy years, have three grown married children. Mary Dian is a Jungian therapist and author of *Four Eternal Women.* They live in Kansas City, Missouri, and are still writing.

Julie L. Moore is a Best of the Net and seven-time Pushcart Prize nominee and the author of four poetry collections, including, most recently, *Full Worm Moon*, which won a 2018 Woodrow Hall Top Shelf Award and received honorable mention for the Conference on Christianity and Literature's 2018 Book of the Year Award. She has also had poetry appear in *Alaska Quarterly Review, African American Review, Image, New Ohio Review, Poetry Daily, Prairie Schooner, The Southern Review, Verse Daily* and *Ruminate*, where she won the Janet B. McCabe Poetry Prize. Moore is the Writing Center Director at Taylor University, where she is the poetry editor for *Relief Journal.*

Angela Alaimo O'Donnell is a professor, poet, and writer at Fordham University in New York City and serves as Associate Director of Fordham's Curran Center for American Catholic Studies. Her publications include two chapbooks and eight collections of poems, among them *Andalusian Hours* (Paraclete, 2020), a collection of 101 poems that channel the voice of Flannery O'Connor; and *Love in the Time of Coronavirus: a Pandemic Pilgrimage* (Paraclete, 2021). O'Donnell has published a prize-winning memoir, *Mortal Blessings* (2014); a book of hours based on the practical theology of Flannery O'Connor, *The Province of Joy* (2012). Her biography, *Flannery O'Connor: Fiction Fired by Faith* (2015), was awarded first prize for excellence in publishing from The Association of Catholic Publishers. Her critical book on Flannery O'Connor, *Radical Ambivalence: Race in Flannery O'Connor,* was published by Fordham University Press in 2020. O'Donnell's most recent poetry collection, *Holy Land,* won the Paraclete Poetry Prize 2021 and was released in October 2022.

Steven Peterson was born in Chicago in 1955. He had a long career as a business writer for an international consulting firm, living in Asia, Europe, and the USA. In 2010 he left that career to write plays and poems. Since then, several of his plays have been produced in theaters around the USA. His poems appear in *America Magazine, The Christian Century, Dappled Things, First Things* and other publications. He is currently a Resident Playwright at Chicago Dramatists. With his wife, Betsy, he lives in Chicago and northern Wisconsin.

Yehiel E. Poupko is Rabbinic Scholar at the Jewish United Fund/Jewish Federation of Metropolitan Chicago. He is an Orthodox rabbi whose poetry is edited by a traditional Lutheran for *The Christian Century*—surely something possible only in the United States. He is the author of *Chana: A Life in Prayer*, and a poetry collection, *What is Lost*.

Donna Pucciani taught English, humanities, music, and women's studies for many years before retiring to write full-time. She has published poetry worldwide in such diverse journals as *Shi Chao Poetry*, *Poetry Salzburg*, *ParisLitUp*, *Acumen*, *The Pedestal*, *Journal of Italian Translation*, *Journal of the American Medical Association*, *Christianity and Literature*, and *America*. Her awards include prizes from the Illinois Arts Council, the National Federation of State Poetry Societies, and Poetry on the Lake (UK/Italy) as well as a number of Pushcart nominations. She was Vice President of Poets Club of Chicago for over a decade. Her seventh and most recent book of poems is *Edges*.

Sarah Rossiter is a writer and a spiritual director. Publications include a novel, *The Human Season*; a short story collection, *Beyond this Bitter Air*; and a poetry chapbook, *Natural Life Without Parole*. Her poetry has appeared in a variety of journals, among them *The Sewanee Review*, *The Southern Review*, *The Anglican Theological Review*, *UU World*, *Sojourners*, and, of course, *The Christian Century*. Mother of four, grandmother of eleven, she lives with her husband in Concord, Massachusetts.

Tania Runyan is the author of the poetry collections *What Will Soon Take Place*, *Second Sky*, *A Thousand Vessels*, *Simple Weight*, and *Delicious Air*, which was awarded Book of the Year by the Conference on Christianity and Literature in 2007. Her first book-length creative nonfiction title, *Making Peace with Paradise: An Autobiography of a California Girl*, was released in 2022. Tania's instructional guides, *How to Read a Poem*, *How to Write a Poem*, and *How to Write a Form Poem*, are used in classrooms across the country, and her poems have appeared in publications such as *Poetry*, *Image*, *Harvard Divinity Bulletin*, *The Christian Century*, and the Paraclete anthology *Christian Poetry in America Since 1940*. Tania was awarded an NEA Literature Fellowship in 2011. She lives with her family in Illinois, where she teaches sixth-grade language arts.

Luci Shaw is Writer in Residence at Regent College, Vancouver. She has authored nearly forty books of poetry and creative non-fiction, and her writing has appeared in numerous literary and religious journals. In 2013 she received the annual Denise Levertov Award for Creative Writing from Seattle Pacific University. Her most recent poetry collection, *Angels Everywhere*, was released in 2022 by Paraclete Press. Her book for children, "The O in Hope," was published by InterVarsity Press in September 2021. Her forthcoming poetry collection, *Reversing Entropy*, will be published by Paraclete Press in 2023.

Barrie Shepherd was UK born and raised, a high school drop-out and RAF veteran. He graduated from the University of Edinburgh and came to the US in 1960 to study at Yale Divinity School. After Yale he served in chaplaincy and teaching at the University of Connecticut, Connecticut College, The College of Wooster, then as senior minister at Swarthmore Presbyterian Church and New York's historic First Presbyterian Church. Shepherd was named William Belden Noble lecturer at Harvard in 1995, and Lyman Beecher lecturer at Yale in 2002. He is the author of eighteen books and is now retired and lives on the Maine coast.

Anya Silver earned a BA from Haverford College and a PhD in Literature from Emory University. She was the author of the poetry collections *Second Bloom* (2017), *From Nothing* (2016), *I Watched You Disappear* (2014), and *The Ninety-Third Name of God* (2010). Her book of literary criticism, *Victorian Literature and the Anorexic Body*, was published in 2006. She was named Georgia Author of the Year for Poetry in 2015 and was awarded a Guggenheim fellowship in 2018. She taught at Mercer University and lived in Georgia until her death in 2018.

Bill Stadick has published poetry, fiction, and creative nonfiction in *The Windhover, Relief, First Things, The Ekphrastic Review, Christianity and Literature* and *The Cresset.* His chapbook, *Family Latin,* was published in January 2020 by Finishing Line Press, and his work has appeared in two anthologies: *Imago Dei: Poems from Christianity and Literature* (Abingdon Press, 2012), and *In a Strange Land: Introducing Ten Kingdom Poets* (Wipf & Stock, 2019).

Bonnie Thurston resigned a Chair and Professorship in New Testament in 2002 to live quietly in her home state of West Virginia. She has written or edited 24 theological books, contributes to scholarly and popular periodicals, authored eight collections of poetry, and published her first poem in *The Christian Century* in 1981. She is an internationally known Thomas Merton Scholar; her doctoral dissertation (University of Virginia) was one of the first on Merton. Bonnie is an avid reader, gardener, cook, walker, and classical music lover.

Shari Wagner is a former Indiana Poet Laureate (2016–2017) and the author of three books of poems: *Evening Chore, The Harmonist at Nightfall,* and, most recently, *The Farm Wife's Almanac.* She lives in Westfield, Indiana, and teaches for Indiana University-Purdue University's Religion, Spirituality, and the Arts Initiative. Her poems have appeared in *American Life in Poetry, The Writer's Almanac, North American Review, Shenandoah,* the anthology *A Cappella: Mennonite Voices in Poetry,* and the Indiana Repertory Theatre's production of *Finding Home: Indiana at 200.* She writes litanies for First Mennonite church of Indianapolis and is at work on a manuscript of poems in the voices of people from Indiana history.

Jeanne Murray Walker was born in a rural village of 900 people in Minnesota and was published by *The Atlantic* at 19. She is the prize-winning author of nine books of poetry, most recently *Pilgrim, You Find the Path by Walking.* Her poems are collected in *Helping the Morning* (WordFarm). Jeanne's poetry and essays have appeared in journals, including *Poetry, Image, The American Poetry Review, The Georgia Review,*

Christian Century, Best American Poetry, and the permanent exhibition at Philadelphia's Comcast Center. Her plays have been produced across the US and in London. She has received many fellowships and 16 nominations for The Pushcart Prize. She served as Mentor in the SPU MFA Program and taught for 40 years at The University of Delaware.

Paul Willis is a professor of English at Westmont College in Santa Barbara, California. He has published seven collections of poetry, the most recent of which is *Somewhere to Follow* (Slant, 2021). He is also the author of an eco-fantasy novel, *The Alpine Tales* (WordFarm, 2010), the YA novel *All in a Garden Green* (Slant, 2020), and the essay collections *Bright Shoots of Everlastingness* (WordFarm, 2005) and *To Build a Trail* (WordFarm, 2018).

Christian Wiman is the author of numerous books, including *My Bright Abyss: Meditation of a Modern Believer*. In 2023 he will publish *Zero at the Bone: Fifty Entries Against Despair*. He teaches at Yale Divinity School.

Carl Winderl has lived, worked, and written in Kyiv, Ukraine; he is currently working in Poland with Ukrainian refugees. Previously he was Professor of Writing at Point Loma Nazarene University in San Diego; he earned a PhD from New York University in Creative Writing and an MA in American Literature from the University of Chicago. Finishing Line Press has published four books of his poems: *Mary Speaks of Her Son* in 2005, *la Via de La Croce* in 2008, *Behold the Lamb* in 2015, and *The Gospel According . . . to Mary* in February, 2021.

IRON PEN

O that my words were written down!
O that they were inscribed in a book!
O that with an iron pen and with lead
they were engraved on a rock forever!
—JOB 19:23–24

Outcast and utterly alone, Job pours out his anguish to his Maker. From the depths of his pain, he reveals a trust in God's goodness that is stronger than his despair, giving humanity some of the most beautiful and poetic verses of all time. Paraclete's Iron Pen imprint is inspired by this spirit of unvarnished honesty and tenacious hope.

OTHER IRON PEN BOOKS

Andalusian Hours, Angela Alaimo O'Donnell

Begin with a Question, Marjorie Maddox

The Consequence of Moonlight, Sofia Starnes

Cornered by the Dark, Harold J. Recinos

Eye of the Beholder, Luci Shaw

Exploring This Terrain, Margaret B. Ingraham

From Shade to Shine, Jill Pelaez Baumgaertner

Glory in the Margins, Nikki Grimes

Idiot Psalms, Scott Cairns

Iona, Kenneth Steven

Litany of Flights, Laura Reece Hogan

Raising the Sparks, Jennifer Wallace

There Is a Future, Amy Bornman

To Shatter Glass, Sister Sharon Hunter, CJ

Wing Over Wing, Julie Cadwallader Staub

About Paraclete Press

Paraclete Press is the publishing arm of the Cape Cod Benedictine community, the Community of Jesus. Presenting a full expression of Christian belief and practice, we reflect the ecumenical charism of the Community and its dedication to sacred music, the fine arts, and the written word.

SCAN
TO
READ
MORE

www.paracletepress.com

Also available from Iron Pen

www.paracletepress.com